Release

to
Grow

Letting Go
Opens The Door
To A New Beginning

Gwengale J. Parker, M. DIV.

authorHOUSE®

AuthorHouse™
1663 Liberty Drive
Bloomington, IN 47403
www.authorhouse.com
Phone: 1 (800) 839-8640

Published by AuthorHouse 01/29/2015

ISBN: 978-1-4969-6754-1 (sc)
ISBN: 978-1-4969-6753-4 (e)

Library of Congress Control Number: 2015901606

Scripture quotations marked KJV are from the Holy Bible, King James
Version (Authorized Version). First published in 1611. Quoted from
the KJV Classic Reference Bible, Copyright © 1983 by The Zondervan
Corporation.

In loving memory of my father, Aaron Jones Sr.; my brother, Reverend Wendell N. Jones; my sister, Marian L. Jones; and my mother, Elestine G. Jones. In the last years of her earthly life, Elestine Gates Jones taught me so much about the importance of knowing how and when to let go of the past. She taught me to treasure the matters of the heart but not allow those treasures to control my destiny. The most important lessons she taught me were to always put God first and to let the love of God be seen in everything I do.

Contents

Foreword

We are living in a season of restlessness. In this season, it is easy to become consumed by unimportant things we believe are very important to our survival. We are becoming more and more consumed with the things of the world. Many have an overwhelming desire to be in total control over what is believed to directly affect their well-being. God revealed this book to me during a very special time in my life. I was busy working in the church, but I still felt empty. I felt as if I was missing something. I wanted more of God. I had an overwhelming desire to move to a higher level in my walk with God. My desire was more than a desire; it was a need that exploded deep within. I needed to feel His presence all the time. The need to be closer to Him and to be a better servant for God grew stronger every day. Instead of praying for God to move me to that place of intimacy with Him, I tried to hold on to where I was. As I desperately grasped for more, I was holding on to things that I needed to release. At the time, I didn't realize I was hindering my spiritual growth by holding on to things from the past.

God showed me that just as I was holding on, there were many people who wanted to be closer to Him but were doing the same thing I was doing. They needed to strengthen their relationships with family members, and they needed to improve the quality of their lives. We often fail at achieving this goal because we don't know what things in our lives we need to release in order to move to the next level. We must let go of the things that are hindering growth. There are times when we have to let go of things and people. We must learn to let go in order to fulfill God's purpose for our lives. We must learn which things to let go of and when to let go of them in order to live our lives fully.

This book encourages self-examination. Are you living your life based upon past hurts and disappointments? Are you looking for approval from others? Are you walking in unforgiveness, hatred, and jealousy? Are you controlled by the desire to gain material items? There comes a time when negative things must be released for growth. There is no way to receive what God has for you if your hands are already full.

On my lunch break, I picked up a large tea, hoping it would last me for the remainder of the workday. When

I first purchased the tea, it was very dark and sweet. As the day progressed, every time I took a sip, the sweetness was fading. By the end of the day, the tea had lightened and lost its sweetness. With time, the tea lost most of its zest. It tasted more like water with a hint of tea and no sugar. Some believers allow their lives to become watered down and diluted by the junk they carry around. The junk causes our thoughts to become those of the world, and they overtake our inner strength. We watch and read things that we should not watch or read. Because our minds become watered down to the ways of the world, we are deceived into believing we are in control of our lives. We should not allow our decisions, mistakes, and feelings of failure to weigh us down. We must release them in order to soar like eagles.

I pray that something in this book will have a positive impact on your life. I pray it will assist you in understanding what things need to be released in order to move to the next level.

Chapter 1
We Are Purposed

Therefore, brethren, we are debtors, not to the
flesh, to live after the flesh. For is we live after the
flesh, ye shall die: but if you through the Spirit do
mortify the deeds of the body, ye shall live.

—Romans 8:12-13

Reading through Romans 8 encouraged me to take a very close look at my life and what God has purposed for me on earth. From our mothers' wombs, we begin with a purpose already set forth by the Creator. How do we know God's divine purpose for our lives? It starts with the ability to hear God. Being in a relationship with Him allows us to know our Master's voice.

Once we hear from God, we must be obedient as we walk in His will. Romans 8:12-13 reminds us that the body is no more than dust. Although we are walking and breathing, we are dying little by little every day. Soon we will dissolve into nothing more than a handful of dirt that will be blown away by the wind. Therefore, we are not to get so caught up in the flesh or things of the flesh. We are not obligated to the flesh because the flesh ties us to the world. We are reminded that our service is to God through our spirit lives. We are not debtors of the flesh; we are debtors of Christ and to the Holy Spirit. Although we all have different callings in our lives, we all have one common purpose. Our first and foremost purpose is to worship and praise God. God put this purpose in place when He created man. Your purpose cannot be known unless you know who you are in Christ.

> And God, said, Let us make man in our image, after our likeness: and let them have dominion over the fish of the sea, and over the fowl of the air, and over the cattle, and over all the earth, and over every creeping thing that creepeth upon the earth. So God created man in his own image, in the image of God created he him; male and female created he them. (Genesis 1:26-27)

God created us in His image. The dictionary defines *image* as a picture or likeness of somebody or something that appears in a mirror. Another definition of image is a person or thing bearing a close likeness to somebody or something else. Therefore, since we are told in the Word of God that man was created in God's image, we were created to display a close likeness to Him. We are purposed to walk, talk, and love others as God loves us. When you love someone, you yearn to spend a lot of time with that person. The more time you spend with that person, the more you need to please him or her. That's how our relationship with God should be. Your love for Him should be the same as His love for you. You should desire a close relationship with Him.

Purpose is defined as the object toward which one strives or for which something exists, an aim, or a goal. Another definition for purpose is something made intentionally and deliberately with good results. God created each of us intentionally and deliberately with good results from His creation. God is the reason we exist and the reason why we exist. God purposed us for divine reasons and earthly reasons. Knowing we were created to worship, we must first understand the purpose of our worship of God.

Our worship must be pleasing to God, and it is what we must do. We must glorify, honor, praise, and exalt God for who He is. Our worship must show adoration and loyalty to God for His grace, which allows us to have that promised eternal life. James 4:6 tells us that we must humble ourselves in the sight of the Lord and He will lift us up. The Word of God tells us to worship God in two ways (John 4:23-24). We must worship in truth and in spirit. As believers, we are not given an option; we must worship the way God has commanded us to.

As children, we all had someone we admired and wanted to be like. I wanted to be like my tenth-grade English teacher. When she spoke, I would hang on every word, admiring the way she articulated the words that flowed from her mouth. She was always dressed in professional attire, and she walked like a model on a runway. She would smile while teaching, and her smile lit up the classroom. I visualized being just like her when I grew up. Sometimes I mimicked the way she carried herself.

I am sure there was someone you admired as well. We should all have the desire and the need to be like our Creator. The only way I could be like my teacher was to study her and put into action the things I learned from her. We become like those we admire and worship. When we admire and worship God, we become like Him. We value what God values, and we take on the characteristics of God.

We can never reach the level of God, but striving to be like him every day gives him much pleasure. Worshipping God gives us the ability to walk in forgiveness, love as God loves, and look for justice. When we do not judge, we display the trait of righteousness.

Understanding our own divine purpose opens the door to understanding our own purpose on earth. Divine purpose is an anchor that secures us as we live a purpose-filled life. Our love for God and our relationship with Him plant the seeds in our hearts to fulfill His purpose for us while we are on earth.

People often ask children what they want to be when they grow up. Some parents and relatives see special talents in them and try to predict what they will be as adults. Few children fulfill these predictions. A person's purpose may or may not include how to make a living. There are many determining factors when it comes to choosing professions. Some decisions are based on how much money people can make, what they enjoy doing, job availability, and the need for an income. Some people work daily in what they are purposed to do.

How can a person know his or her purpose? I like to think of purpose as a matter of the heart. It is an unexplained burning desire that pierces the heart to the point that it needs to be satisfied. This craving makes you cry out to God and say, "Yes, Lord. I will go. Send me."

Your purpose is what comes naturally to you. You do it without a single thought. Walking in your purpose may look foolish to others. Sometimes you don't even understand why you do it. Walking in your purpose means walking in faith. Knowing who you are and who you belong to makes walking in your purpose much easier.

Noah walked in his purpose. He was purposed by God to build the ark. It didn't matter how foolish he looked building an ark and never seeing rain. He may have looked foolish to others, but he was obedient and trusted God by staying true to his purpose. Moses could not talk plainly, but God purposed him to lead His people. He may have gotten weary, disappointed, confused along the way, but he lived the purpose God called him for. God purposed Mary, the mother of Jesus, to carry His Son. God purposed David to be a great leader from a very early age.

There is no way we can understand or walk in our purposes if we are carrying around a lot of unnecessary baggage. Baggage filled with things we don't need and things that do not belong to us. When we walk in our purposes, God is pleased with us. Are you walking in your purpose? Does your life reflect who you are in Christ? We all have power, and we must channel it into energy for a purpose.

Chapter 2

A Divine Invitation

For God so loved the world, that He gave his
only begotten Son, that whoever believeth in him
should not perish, but have everlasting life.
—John 3:16

This is wonderful news for you and me. God loves us so much that He gave the life of His Son, Jesus Christ, so we could have wonderful lives on earth and for all of eternity.

We are such blessed people. My heart overflows with joy and praise every time I think about God giving us such a divine gift. We are undeserving, but God saw fit to give us such a prodigious gift. Every time we think of God and the gift he has given us, we need to stop, take a moment, and thank Him for His goodness.

Unfortunately, life's activities and the unnecessary things we concern ourselves with have caused us to grow slack and apathetic when it comes to getting in touch with our spiritual beings. When God created us, He knew we would stray from His Word because we get so involved with things and concerns of this world that we leave our first love. Our first love is God. We are drawn away from our first love because we spend too much time holding onto the things we don't need while endeavoring to attain things we really don't need.

"Nevertheless, I have somewhat against thee because thou hast left my first love" (Revelation 2:4). When believers first dedicate their lives to God, they are on fire. They are ready to do anything to build God's kingdom. They take advantage of every opportunity to study and learn more about living a spirit-filled life. Over time, the thirst and hunger evaporates just as water in a well dries up. Over time, new believers find themselves disconnected from God. They focus on the things of the world and what the world says is right. They get comfortable with the things of the world. They sometimes turn away from God and begin packing their bags with a lot of unnecessary stuff.

Separation from God is like a marriage that has gone bad. Think back to when you first met the love of your life, the person you wanted to spend the rest of your life with. When you first met, you couldn't get enough of each other.

You talked on the phone for endless hours, never concerning yourself with how long the telephone calls lasted. You would take advantage of any opportunity to spend time together. You yearned to learn as much about each other as you could. When you spent time with friends, you didn't mind going on and on about the wonderful person in your life. You talked about the wonderful relationship you were building and your plans for the future.

After being in the relationship for a period of time, things began to change. The fire that was burning in your heart was gradually extinguished. Your conversations became shorter and shorter. You no longer cared about spending time together. Before you realized what was happening, your relationship no longer existed. You and your soul mate slowly drifted apart, leaving you both wondering when you stopped loving and caring for each other.

Just as relationships end, the same happens in our relationships with God. We come to God on fire. We accept him as our Lord and Savior. You talk to Him for countless hours and take every opportunity to learn more about Him. We long for more of Him and love spending every moment with him. Jobs, social events, family activities, and the desire for material gain come before Him. Before you realize it, conversations with Him are far and few between. There is no longer a burning desire to learn more about Him. The things of the world have caused a separation. You are left alone, and you wonder what went wrong. You wonder when it went wrong. You are no longer in a relationship with your first love.

When God gives me a writing assignment, I take it very seriously. With this book and my previous books, I spent a lot of time praying and fasting about the message He wanted to convey through me. I know that order is very important when there is a message to be related.

My mind told me that this chapter was to be last, but God said it should be the second chapter. Because His ways and thoughts are higher than mine, I didn't understand. I know I have to be obedient to God and keep His order. God spoke to me and said, "Yes, this book is about releasing. There is something I have already given my people they need to be reminded of."

Reminding them first will enhance the need and the understanding about the importance of releasing. First, we are to be reminded of a very special invitation that God has given us. Most people, including churchgoers, have forgotten this invitation. He gave it to us because He loves us. When the releasing process is taking place, we will remember receiving the invitation. Once we remember receiving the invitation, we will want to go back, retrieve it, and get dressed for the occasion. This invitation has been extended to all—rich, poor, young, old—regardless of nationality. Most read and accept the invitations, but they carelessly discard them. Others overlook them like pieces of junk mail. Other people forget about the invitations. There were no dates on the invitations, and people didn't have to RSVP. People overlooked the invitations for whatever reasons, but most felt the invitations didn't need to be answered until the end of their lives.

We must spend every day of our lives preparing ourselves to accept God's divine invitation.

> And Jesus answered and spake unto them again by parables, and said, The kingdom of heaven is like unto a certain king, which made a marriage for his son, And sent forth his servants to call them that were bidden to the wedding: and they would not come. Again, he sent forth other servants, saying, tell them which are bidden, Behold, I have prepared my dinner: my oxen and my fatlings are killed, All things are ready: come unto the marriage. But they made light of it, and went their ways, one to his farm, another to his merchandise: And the remnant took his servants, and entreated them spitefully And slew them. But when the king heard thereof, he was wroth: and he sent forth his armies, and destroyed those murders, and burned up their city. Then saith he to his servants, the wedding

is ready, but they which were bidden were not worthy. Go ye therefore unto the highways, and gathered together all as many as they found both bad and good: and the wedding was furnished with guests. And when the king came to see the guests he say there a man which had not on a wedding garment: And he saith unto him, Friend, how camest thou in hither not having a wedding garment and he was speechless, Then said the king to the servants, bind him hand and foot, and take him away, and cast him unto outer darkness; there shall be weeping and gnashing of teeth. For many are called but few are chosen. (Matthew 22:1-14)

Jesus told this parable about His coming kingdom. In the scriptures, Jesus told of a king who sent his servants out with invitations to his son's wedding celebration. The first invitations were sent to certain people, but they did not accept the invitations. The king sent his servants out again to personally deliver the invitations and tell them that a great feast had been prepared. The invitations went out as urgent messages.

The king said, "Let them know I have killed my best oxen and fatling. Everything is ready. Come on. Be partakers of the feast I have prepared."

When the king said everything is ready, that let the receivers of the invitations know they needed to prepare and get there as soon as possible. Instead of paying close attention to the invitations and taking time to understand the message, they discarded it. They also killed the servants who delivered the invitations.

The king was so upset about the rejection of his servants that he ordered his servants to destroy the murderers. He also burned their cities. The king made one last attempt to get someone to share in the wedding celebration. The invitation was now open to anyone: the good, the evil, and the unworthy. Those deemed unworthy accepted the invitations, and the house of the king was filled. One thing that occurred at the feast really stood out to me. One man was not dressed for the occasion. Because he was not dressed for the occasion, he was bound hand and feet and cast out into the darkness. The Word predicted weeping and gnashing of teeth. That let me know that rejecting the invitation and accepting the invitation without dressing for it comes with a price.

The man who was not dressed for the occasion knew he was not prepared to attend the great celebration. In order to get in, he pretended to be something he was not. Today, many people are loaded down with stuff. The stuff in our lives keeps us from accepting the divine invitation. We try to look like we are dressed for the wedding celebration, but our hearts are full of stuff that needs to be released. It is important to understand we must be dressed and prepared to walk in the king's presence if we plan to accept the invitation.

God invited everyone to a great celebration. God was preparing a wedding celebration for His Son. He charged His servants with delivering invitations to the masses. Because of the nature of the invitations, some of His servants will be accused, misunderstood, and abused. In spite of the dangers that come with the charge, the invitations must be delivered. There are no dates on the invitations, and you don't have to RSVP.

Saying yes to the divine invitation is saying yes to accepting your place at the wedding supper of our Lord. Everyone is invited, but no one is forced to attend. If you plan to attend, you must do what the invitation says. You must prepare. It does not matter what clothes you wear to cover your flesh. Your soul must be dressed, and you must be prepared in order to attend.

"I am delivering an invitation from on high. Come to the marriage of the lamb." If you plan on attending, there is an urgent need to start dressing for the occasion right now. Start releasing yourself from being consumed by worldly issues. Focus on the origin of the greatest invitation you will ever receive. Preparing this celebration cost God the life and blood of Jesus Christ. God has promised to feed the dying with the power of a heavenly life. The lost will be restored, and those who thirst after Him will be satisfied with Him.

Are you planning to attend the wedding of the Lamb of God? Don't be like the man who was bound, rejected, and tossed into darkness because he was not dressed for the occasion. Dressing for the wedding of the Lamb of God means preparing your soul. Those who do not have a saving relationship with Jesus Christ will not be prepared. Those who are burdened with unnecessary stuff of this world will not be prepared. They will be cast into darkness. To attend the feast, you must:

- remove idols of the heart (Genesis 35:2-5)
- walk in forgiveness (Mark 11:25)
- consecrate your home (Exodus 19:10)
- reconcile with those you have offended (Matthew 5:23-24)
- love one another (1 John 3:16)
- develop a love relationship with the Father (John 14:23)

I am excited about the invitation God has extended to me. When I read John 14:1-6, my soul rejoices at the comforting words of Jesus. The scripture gives me hope and joy. These words assure me of my eternal future:

> Let not your heart be troubled; ye believe in
> God, believe also in me. In my Father's house
> are many mansions if it were not so, I would
> have told you. I go to prepare a place for you.
> And if I go and prepare a place for you, I will
> come again and receive you unto myself; that
> where I am there ye may be also. And whither
> I go ye know, and the way ye know. Thomas
> saith unto him, Lord, we know not whither
> thou goest; and how can we know the way?
> Jesus saith unto him, I am the way, the truth,
> and the life; no man cometh unto the Father
> but by me. (John 14:1-6)

We often hear this scripture when someone dies, but these are encouraging words for the living. Jesus told us what awaits us in our eternal lives. These encouraging words should make us want to strive to remove the foolishness of the world and be about the heavenly Father's business. Put aside the stuff you are carrying—whether it is your stuff or someone else's stuff. Put it all aside so that you are free to move to the next level.

Strive to attain only what God has planned for you. Release the stuff that is keeping you from living a life of purpose. Release the stuff that will keep you from attending the wedding celebration of the Lamb of God. Release the stuff that is keeping you from seeing the promise that God made to us.

We must prepare ourselves for the celebration. We must be worthy of eating and drinking with the Lord. God is not forcing himself on anyone; the choice is ours. Examine yourself. Are you worthy of sitting at His table, or are you caught up in stuff?

Chapter 3

Baggage Check

A young man packed his bags as his young daughter looked on. It was a weekly routine because the father's job required him to travel on weekdays. He returned home on Fridays. As the father packed his bags, the young child watched with confusion. She said, "If you are only going to be gone four days, why do you need so much stuff?"

He explained how he needed work clothes for the week and how he might need additional clothing. He searched for other items to place in the bags. When the packing was complete, the father had three pieces of luggage. He also had two additional bags for his computer and other electronic gadgets.

The next morning, the father departed for the airport. He sprinted through the airport because he was a running a little behind. He checked three of the bags, which left him with a computer case and the one filled with gadgets. He placed his Bluetooth in his ear, browsed through his e-mail, and answered text messages.

When he arrived at the airport, he was carrying a lot of baggage. Once he checked his baggage, his load was lighter. The bags he kept were distracting him from paying close attention to his surroundings. He took a minute to rearrange the bags before he boarded the plane. On the plane, he put his bags in the overhead compartment and took his seat. At last, he was able to sit back and not worry about keeping up with his stuff for the duration of the flight.

Once he reached his destination, he would have to pick up his bags again. He was relieved not to be struggling for a short period of time. He had a chance to leave the airport without his bags. Leaving the bags behind would give him an opportunity to start fresh. He could purchase the things he needed for the rest of his trip.

His daughter's question echoed in his ears: *Daddy, why do you need so much stuff?*

He began to wonder if he truly needed all the items he packed. He thought about some of the unnecessary items in his bags. He didn't really need all those things. He realized they were weighing him down.

At his destination, he collected his baggage from the baggage claim. The weight of the bags was unbearable. He searched anxiously for a car rental company so he could relieve himself of carrying around the baggage. He vowed never to pack so many items. He would only pack the things he would be using. He had brought some items he thought might be useful to some of his coworkers. He was carrying his weight—and the weight of others.

At the hotel, he began to unpack his bags. His daughter's voice still rang in his ears. He wondered why he had packed so much stuff. As he sorted through his bag, it became obvious that he could have made the trip with only one bag. Packing only what was necessary would have been so much easier. The young man's bag was filled with unnecessary stuff.

Just as the man packed his bags with unnecessary stuff, we too pack our bags with unnecessary stuff. This unnecessary stuff causes us to focus on the stuff—and lose focus of God's purpose for our lives. We start our days by packing our bags and readying ourselves for whatever our days hold. We pack our bags with stuff that does not belong to us. We pack our bags with stuff we decide to take from others. We pack our bags with things we can't do anything about.

I realize most of us don't pack to take an actual trip every day. The bags represent our spirits. When we wake up daily, we renew our spirits with stuff that we need desperately to release. As believers, we must understand the importance of letting go and letting God. God wants to bless each of us and take us to new levels, but we choose to hold on to the stuff that stunts our growth. The stuff clutters our minds and hardens our hearts.

There was one thing the man did not have to encounter. Even though he had a lot of stuff in his bags, he didn't have to deal with a baggage search. Unlike the man, most of us have to be searched because of what we have in our bags.

At the baggage checkpoint, it is brought to the official's attention that some things in our bags cannot be taken on the plane. There are some things in our spirits that we cannot take to the wedding celebration. God has rejected the items in our spirits, and they must be disposed of.

A person may wake up with a filthy mouth, an attitude of quarreling, discord, resentment, pride, strife, jealousy, malice, a lying or gossiping tongue, thoughts of persecution, a spirit of superiority, or prejudices. A person may wake up with a controlling spirit, a judgmental spirit, or a self-righteous spirit. Others may wake up with bitterness in their hearts, anger, arrogance, anxiety, hatred, unforgiveness, unbelief, or revenge. Others battle fears of rejection, persecution, criticism, injustice, or faultfinding. Some people in your bags need to be removed. The list goes on and on.

We all need to take some time to look in our bags before we reach the officials. First, we must identify the stuff in our bags. We must sort everything—just as we sort laundry that needs to be washed. Once we have identified the stuff, we must decide what's important and what will enhance our growth. Is there something in your bag that can be considered dead weight? After digging into my bags, I found some stuff I didn't realize was in there. Many people spend lifetimes thinking they have it all together. A closer look reveals that there are things in your bags you didn't know were there. Some stuff has been in the bags so long that it's going to take some hard work to remove.

Before starting this book, I interviewed ten people of various ages, genders, and races. I asked, "What in your life do you need to release?"

They all gave similar answers—with the exception of two women. One young lady needed to release hatred that stemmed from disappointment. She was disappointed that her father was never there when she needed him. Her disappointment caused her to have hatred in her heart for her father. Because of that hatred, she was unable to maintain healthy relationships. She felt rejected because of a failed marriage. Another said she needed to release a misunderstanding that kept her from having a relationship with her sister. Most people had personal issues they needed to release. Some needed to release the need for material gain.

One young lady needed to release some recent experiences with family members. A young man needed to release traditions he learned in church. The answers dealt with healing from a personal perspective, which started with an inward healing of the heart. The statement about traditions in church dealt directly with his personal relationship with God. After praying about the statement, I understood what he meant. All churches govern themselves through rituals and traditions. At times, we get caught up in *worshipping* traditions instead of *honoring* traditions.

What's the difference between worshipping traditions and honoring traditions? There is a fine line between the two, but they are definitely different. Tradition is defined as the handing down of beliefs, opinions, or customs. In churches and other places of worship, practices are passed down from one generation to another. Denominations pass down traditions that originated with our forefathers.

The definition of *worship* is to pay great honor to what is considered extremely precious. Honor is defined as respect or courtesy. Christians should not be worshipping traditions. Worshipping traditions means we are worshipping the practices that are passed down to us. God is the only one who deserves to be worshipped. We need to give God the honor of our worship. We should honor traditions by respecting what the traditions represent. Because of our love for God, we should respect the traditions as a reminder of who He is to us and what He has done for us. Many people attend church out of tradition or because it is the right thing to do. Many traditions hinder spiritual growth within the church. We have no idea why so many are in place. The worshipping traditions of the church need to be reevaluated.

On my daily route to work, I pass a small business that is located on a busy highway. The owner of the business always takes the time to post weekly inspirations on the signboard in front of the business. Some are original, and others are familiar. As I approach the business, I glance at the signboard. One day, the posting said, "God don't make no junk."

I thought, *How familiar. I have seen this statement a lot.*

As I continued on my commute, my thoughts kept going back to the signboard.

God spoke to me and said, "I don't make no junk, but people make junk."

God doesn't make junk, but man does a wonderful job of it. We think junk, talk junk, associate with junk, and do junky things. Man turns what God made good into junk. When junk or unnecessary stuff penetrates the minds and hearts of men and women, their souls become infested. An infestation of the soul is separation from God. God cannot take us to that place He has purposed for us if that place is filled with junky stuff.

The stuff in our lives holds our spirits hostage. Many want to break free, but they don't know what to release or how to start the releasing process. Living a life filled with stuff is like going through life with your hands tied together. It limits the ability to function. You twist and turn, but you are not able to break free. The more you twist and turn, the more frustrated you become. A lot of movement without going anywhere is the same as a lot of useless motions. When you get tired of being bound, you make one last attempt to free yourself. When you make that one powerful motion, you are able to break free.

The same applies to the stuff in our lives. We must free ourselves from some things. Some things rob us of peaceful, purposeful lives on earth. As we move into the next chapters, join me as I start unpacking my bags.

Chapter 4

The Wounded Can Be Healed

When bags are packed with unnecessary stuff, it opens the door for negativity. *Stuff* is the reason for the pain we endure. We get caught up in the memories of things that have caused us pain. Allowing yourself to get caught up in the memories will infest the mind and heart and allow the hurt to continue to grow. Replaying painful memories results in bitterness, fear, and rejection. These feelings are unwarranted. Placing your trust in God through Jesus Christ can heal the wounds of your broken spirit and give you perfect peace.

> And the peace of God, which passeth all understanding, shall keep your hearts and minds through Christ Jesus. (Philippians 4:7)

Thou wilt keep him in perfect peace, whose mind is stayed on thee: Because he trusteth in thee. (Isaiah 26:3)

We are wounded in so many ways: words, evil doings, untruths, misunderstandings, confusion, broken hearts, hatred, mistreatment, grief, and disappointment. We carry these things in our broken spirits. These things are inflicted upon us by people in the workplace, in society, at home, and in church. Family members and those we consider friends have put some of the unnecessary stuff in our bags.

The pain is transfixed in the mind like a scene in a horror movie. Memories need to be healed so the heart and spirit can be healed. Bad memories of people, places, things, and events can make you tremble. Bad memories can cause sickness, restless nights, and the inability to function normally. Spiritual healing must take place because we all deserve to be freed from bad memories. We must deal with bad memories by using our minds, wills, and emotions. Memories release poison gases in our spirit. They are like a mass explosion of bitterness, rejection, fear, and condemnation.

Even though bad memories run through our minds, bodies, and souls, healing is possible. We must have the desire to be freed from the bondage of bad memories. It is important to feast upon the Word of God. Look for the positive in the midst of the negative as you build new memories. "He healeth the broken in heart and bindeth up their wounds" (Psalm 147:3).

Affliction is defined as any condition or problem that produces pain or suffering. Sorrow is defined as extreme sadness or mental distress. Affliction can be caused by words, misunderstandings, mistreatment, feeling unloved, a failed marriage, abuse, neglect, or disappointment. These things can also cause sorrow and grief in a person's heart. Affliction and sorrow never go unnoticed by God. "Surely, he hath borne our grief, and carried our sorrows" (Isaiah 53:4).

Understanding there is a comforter in all our discomforts is the first step to healing our wounded spirits. "But the Comforter which is the Holy Ghost, whom the Father will Send in my name, he shall teach you all things, and bring all things to your remembrance, whatsoever I have said unto you" (John 14:26).

Establishing a solid relationship with God and being faithful to His Word will open the door to healing all your wounded memories. We must know that we can hide under God's loving wings of protection. Placing your trust in Him will provide a place of refuge along with the peace and joy that the soul longs for.

The Lord recompense they work, and a full reward be given thee of the Lord God of Israel, under whose wings thou art come to trust. (Ruth 2:12)

Keep me as an apple of the eye, hide me under the shadow of thy wings. (Psalm 17:8)

Be merciful unto me, O God, be merciful unto me: for my soul trusteth in thee: yea, in the shadow of thy wings will I make my refuge, until these calamities be overpast. (Psalm 57:1)

I will abide in thy tabernacle forever: I will trust in the covert of Thy wings. (Psalm 61:4)

Because thou hast been my help, therefore in the shadow of thy Wings will I rejoice. (Psalm 63:7)

Whatever the cause for brokenness, we all seem to have some type of connection with rejection. We must understand that God loves all of us. When we come to the realization of God's love for us, there is stability in our lives. Walking in rejection brings feelings of inadequacy. Rejection is a sickness that comes with many ailments. Insecurity fuels fear, guilt, the need to run away from reality, and self-rejection. Fear is common when rejection is involved. Rejection brings expectations of more rejection.

Other ailments that come with rejection are rebellion and self-pity. When all seems hopeless, look to God. The love of God will help the hopeless find hope.

Many are left with the pain of the church's rejection, and some feel rejected by deceased loved ones. Rejection brings the sinful nature of fear. Living in fear of rejection causes people to live in the expectation of continued rejection. The Word of God tells us He is not present where there is fear. Instead of maintaining rejection in your bag, remove it—and replace it with love.

When a person is rejected, that person usually battles self-rejection. Choosing to walk in love helps in the beginning healing process. Love casts out the wounded spirit of rejection.

"There is no fear in love, but perfect love casteth out fear Because fear hath torment" (1 John 4:18). The spirit of rejection must be released because it causes so many other problems that sojourn a purpose-filled life. The worst effect of rejection is a heart of hardness. A heart of hardness removes the ability to be compassionate. The inability to forgive is the main reason so many carry around unnecessary baggage. Unforgiveness is the root of hurt, disappointment, harden hearts, and hatred. We can equate unforgiveness with wounded spirits—no matter what the underlying reasons may be. There is healing for the wounded that begins with forgiveness.

Healing starts with the forgiveness of others—and forgiveness of yourself. A woman can forgive her father for not being in her life, but she must forgive herself for not allowing herself to receive or give love. Forgiving the offending party is the only acceptable response to God. Forgiving yourself is forgiving what you regret doing—and not allowing yourself to live a purpose-filled life. People must open their hearts and be willing to forget the things of the past if they want to live in the present. Only releasing can heal the wounded.

> Brethren, I count not myself to have apprehended: but this One thing I do, forgetting those things which are behind, and Reaching forth unto those things which are before. (Philippians 3:13)

To count is to take inventory. We must take inventory of ourselves in order to know what needs to be released. To apprehend is to obtain. We must take inventory in order to attain healing for our wounds.

Philippians 3:13 explains how we must forget in order to move ahead. We have to look forward to move forward. My brother I took inventory of myself. I have counted all the things in life that shouldn't be there. I have not obtained perfection, but I have decided to leave behind the things of the past. I choose to leave the things of the past behind and press on toward the mark. I realize my wounded spirit can be healed, but first I had to make the choice to release the things in my life I didn't need.

When people are faced with rejection, they either react or respond. How rejection is handled is based on the character of the individual. Individuals who react are moved by what they see, hear, and feel. They move in opposition to the forces at hand. Reacting causes emotional disorder to a life situation. Individuals answer for their actions. They choose right over wrong. Reacting is the way of the world, but responding is knowing and trusting God.

The wounded can be healed through releasing. The release comes when you bring the things in your life that need to be released into the light of God. Once they are brought into the light, turn the issues over to God. Ask God to give you what you need to release those issues—and do not pick them up again. The things needing to be released from your life are things of the dark. When the light of God shines over you, the darkness is no longer there. Darkness and light cannot coexist. Release means bad situations or people that cause you pain will no longer hold you hostage in the darkness.

Wounds are healed when you enter an intimate relationship with God. Turn your heart to God, take off your mask, and understand who you are. Tell God how you feel—and open yourself up for the power of God to move in your life. "But seek ye first the kingdom of God, and his righteousness; and all these things shall be added unto you" (Matthew 6:33).

Make sure the first thing you do is look to the kingdom of God for His power and righteousness; and what you petition God for will be granted to you. "Choose you this day whom ye will serve, as for me and my house we will serve the Lord" (Joshua 24:15).

Making the decision to choose to serve God is the beginning of the rebuilding process. You are then able to see yourself as God sees you. Know God loves you. He does not want you to be burdened by unnecessary stuff. If you have picked up stuff, drop it. If you have taken on stuff that belongs to someone else, give it back. It's not yours to carry. If there is someone in your life who you considered a friend, but he or she is holding you back, walk away. Press on alone.

If you are misunderstood in your words or actions, step away, talk to God, and do His will. He made you. He understands you and knows the sincerity of your actions. The wounded can be healed through releasing. The power starts within you. Jesus can—and will—break every chain that binds you.

Chapter 5
Release To Grow

In the past chapters, I have mentioned forgiveness on several occasions. I believe that we can only be released by walking in forgiveness. Forgiveness and freedom go hand in hand. Releasing to grow begins with establishing a relationship with God through His Son Jesus Christ. Having the inability to release means maintaining the inability to forgive. The ability to forgive means living in peace and joy in Jesus Christ. Forgiveness is restoring something that is lost and reconnecting in fellowship. In order to live purposeful lives, we must restore what we have lost within ourselves. And once we learn to come into fellowship, we understand the meaning of a purpose-filled life.

Forgiveness is a very deep work for God. I like to refer to forgiveness as God performing open-heart surgery on a broken heart. During this surgery, He opens up the heart, exposing everything that is wrong with it. The heart is open, and the sickness of the heart is revealed. Once a diagnosis is made, God starts to repair the heart. God repairs the damage that has been done to the heart. Once He has closed the wound, it's up to the individual to go through the healing process. After the surgery, there will be pain. Just because the master surgeon performed the surgery does not mean you come out of surgery ready to tackle the world. The healing process involves time and endurance. During the open-heart surgery, God implants forgiveness. Now that forgiveness has been implanted, the healing process involves understanding the new implant.

Forgiveness is the way in, and reconciliation is the way to accomplish the releasing of power. Forgiveness does not always restore relationships, but it restores the heart of someone who needs to release bitterness.

The first issue Jesus addressed with the disciples after His resurrection shows us how to enter into the power of forgiving. Jesus started his teachings with a declaration of peace and ended with a profound statement about the forgiveness of sins. "Whosesoever sins remit they are remitted unto them: they are remitted unto them and whosoever sins ye retain they are retained" (John 20:23). This presents us with a challenge concerning forgiveness.

Scripture tells us what we must do. If we forgive others for their sins, they are forgiven. If we do not forgive others for their sins, they are not forgiven. How can an individual have the power of forgiveness in his or her hands? It is important to know that Jesus's statement in this verse is not dealing with forgiveness from the eternal aspect. This statement addresses justification toward other people. The unforgiveness some people hold against us does not interfere with their justification before God through Jesus Christ.

> Then said Jesus to them again. Peace be unto you as my Father hath sent me, even so send I you. And when he had said this, he breathed on them, and saith unto them, receive ye the Holy Ghost. (John 20:12-22)

Jesus breathed His life into the disciples, and He breathed His life into us as believers.

Having received a part of His life, we are authorized to operate under the power of God. Jesus made the provision for forgiveness by presenting His blood at the throne of God. We were granted peace, which means we were reconciled. It is by way of the cross that we are reconciled to God. There is no way possible for us to have peace apart from the place where peace has been made. The cross is where our peace begins.

The inability to forgive has caused broken homes, broken families, hatred, abuse, rebellion, rejection, and other negative spirits. We must learn to forgive if we want to break the chains that bind us. God accepted the blood of His Son as atonement for the sins of the world. While hanging on that old rugged cross, just before taking his last breath, Jesus asked his Father to "forgive them." We must do as Jesus did and remember God's kingdom is not built on unforgiveness.

Humans have different characteristics. We are not expected to see eye to eye on every issue that comes before us, but we are expected to respect everyone's right to be who they are and resolve our differences through love. As His children, we are called to demonstrate His forgiveness of sins. The decision to walk in forgiveness is one the best gifts we can give back to God.

As believers, we have the power to bind or free other people. We can set the captive free by forgiving—or we can bind through the power of unforgiveness. To forgive our brothers and sisters is the breaking of chains. If we continue to walk in unforgiveness, we will hold all people hostage forever.

I once believed that God was the only one whose forgiveness mattered. My study of forgiveness revealed to me that we as believers are the church on earth. The church is not a building; it is the love of Jesus within the believers' hearts. Since we are the church, the church was established through us. We are granted the power to carry on as Jesus did. The power we have been given reaches into heaven, the kingdom where the evils of Satan are working constantly to resist God.

> Again I say unto you. That if two of you shall agree on earth as touching anything that they shall ask, it shall be done for them of my Father which is in heaven. (Matthew 18:19)

The power we have against the evils of this world is an agreement we have when we are walking in forgiveness with one another. We set our brothers and sisters free so that Satan is the one who is bound. On the other hand, if we choose to bind our brothers and sisters, we set Satan free. Setting Satan free gives him access to roam and destroy the world. Satan's freedom is an open door for a life of corruption and disappointment.

Unforgiveness comes with a big price tag. The inability to forgive burdens us and causes us to become tormentors of guilt, fear, hatred, and physical problems. God does not call for unconditional forgiveness because He is not aware of what has been done to us. God created forgiveness to release us from the torment of injustices, negative emotions, hurtful relationships, resentment, and the torment of our own personalities. When it comes to trusting and having faith in God, too many believers are simply going through the motions as they walk in confusion. Many are just going through the motions. God does not want us going through the motions. He intended for us to live a free, purposeful lives as his children. He wants us to have free minds and spirits on this earth. He knew we would face unjustifiable circumstances, and that's why we have been granted the provision of forgiveness.

We must have the attitude of Jesus's heart. This attitude is not based on what people do to you or what others are doing. It is based upon an individual's need for redemption. We must draw from the heart of Jesus. His love swallows all hatred. When wronged, we must learn to say, "Father forgive them." If we hold each other in prisons of unforgiveness, who will reap the harvest? A forgiving heart demonstrates our cooperation with the scriptural injunction to esteem our brothers and sister more highly than ourselves.

There is an order when it comes to forgiveness. First, we must examine ourselves to determine if we recognize the unforgiveness in ourselves. Sometimes the inability to forgive is buried so deep that it is hard for us to see. We call it everything but unforgiveness. With our mouths, we may speak the words of forgiveness, but deep in our hearts, we do not forgive. In our hearts, we do not release others from our negative feelings, thoughts, and attitudes. Forgiveness is like cleaning a house; after a general cleaning, we have to maintain the cleanliness. To maintain a spirit of forgiveness, we must search our minds and hearts daily.

There are several types of forgiveness.

False Forgiveness

These thoughtless deceptions lead us to believe that we have forgiven when we have not. False forgiveness counterfeits the work of the spirit. To put it another way, you say you forgive someone, but your heart is still burdened with unforgiveness. We speak forgiveness to let someone off the hook or to ease our consciences. True forgiveness reopens the lines of communication until our hearts are in touch with each other again. False forgiveness may pierce the ears, but the hearts never reconnect.

Whole Forgiveness

This process is divided into three parts: forgiveness, reconciliation, and restoration. The parable of the prodigal son is an excellent example of forgiveness. The son hurt his father very much. In spite of being hurt, the father's heart was full of love and compassion for his son. Because of his love for the son, when the son returned, the father forgave him and welcomed him with open arms. When the son returned home, the father did not remind him of what he had done. The father did not hesitate at all to forgive. He ran to meet the son and gave him the best robe, ring, and shoes he had. The most remarkable thing was what he did first that allows us to see forgiveness in action. He greeted his son with a kiss that restored his son's heart as if he had never left home. Can you be as forgiving as the father even if you are not guaranteed that things will go your way? The answer to this question has everything to do with the way you love God.

Halfway Forgiveness

I am sure that all of us at some time or another have been in contact with someone who halfway forgave someone. I am referring to the person who has been hurt by another. Every time you see that person, he or she relives the history of the hurt. The person always speaks about how he or she was wronged but were able to forgive anyway. When you totally forgive someone, there is no need or desire to continue to talk about the occurrence. Halfway forgiveness begins the process of whole forgiveness, but it stops short of completing the process. Halfway forgiveness is just as bad as not forgiving at all. It leaves the person needing forgiveness hanging in limbo.

Heart Forgiveness

Heart forgiveness is when people find a way to forgive—from the heart—someone who is very close to them. Heart forgiveness determines the condition of the heart. Whether or not we truly love the person, we say we have forgiven. Heart forgiveness requires much faith. In this situation, you must believe that God enters the situation with the purpose of changing the situation. When Moses and the children of Israel came to the bitter waters, God showed Moses a tree to cast into the bitter water, which made the water fit to drink. We can't change the circumstances of our bitter situations, but we can change what the situations mean. When matters of the heart come into play, forgiveness is hard. These situations can easily turn into hatred. In order to get to the place God wants us to be, we must allow God to shed the light of the Holy Spirit on us.

My mother loved to bake. When she would prepare to bake a cake, she did it in order. She would take out her special recipe because she did not want to get the recipe wrong. It was important that she baked the best cake for her family. She would take time to gather the right ingredients and combine them just as the recipe instructed. When it was time to combine the ingredients, she would take out her cake mixer. After ensuring the mixer was on the right speed, she would blend all the ingredients together. The right ingredients in the correct order brought good results. Consider handling the act of forgiveness in this way. Take the ingredients—confrontation, persuasion, discipline, love, kindness, and compassion—and place them in your heart. Blend them together until they are mixed well because the combination provides the best results. My mother would place her cake in the oven for a certain amount of time. One you have combined the ingredients for forgiveness in your heart, step back and let God do the cooking.

When the cake comes out the oven, if you followed the directions, the results are good. When you go into the fire and God brings you out, there can be nothing but good results. When you come out of the fire, you will have regained the self-confidence that was lost in unforgiveness. Your perspective has changed; all self-condemnation is gone. You are given a lifetime of redemption through the blood of Jesus. Walking in forgiveness is the key to releasing the unnecessary stuff in your life. It allows you to move to the next level.

There is no way to hold the hurts of the past in our hearts and move to the next level. Forgiveness is a cleansing of the mind, body, and soul, and it opens the door to a healthier lifestyle. The release of old stuff that clutters your spirit will open doors and restore relationships.

Before closing this chapter, I would like to share a wonderful testimony of forgiveness. I was talking with a friend about the need to forgive in order to move to the next level. It is important for spiritual growth and our personal lives. With several shared testimonies of forgiveness, there was one that really touched my heart.

This is a testimony of forgiveness about a small church in the inner city. The church was established many years ago. It had an average of more than one hundred members. The small church was stable. They were financially blessed for a congregation of its size. There had been only three pastors to lead the church. It found itself in an unforeseen turmoil. God allowed the finances of the church to grow, making it possible for them to move forward in the building of God's kingdom. For no apparent reason, the church began to struggle financially. It was later revealed that the pastor was embezzling from the church. The pastor was looked upon as a righteous man of God. How could someone who was highly respected and entrusted to lead the congregation steal from God? This was hard to accept and understand.

Once the wrong was revealed, emotions and unforgiveness came into play. A lot of hurtful things were said, and a lot of ill feelings surfaced. Needless to say, the pastor left the church in disarray. After months of searching for a new leader, the church made a decision to call a new leader. The new pastor accepted the call, but he had conditions. He told the congregation that God revealed to him the church was in a state of confusion because of ill feelings toward the past pastor. He told them that before the church could move to the next level, they had to make a combined effort to forgive the past pastor. He explained that God would hold the past pastor accountable for his wrongdoing. The church members had an obligation to forgive him and free themselves.

After a period of fasting and praying, everyone agreed to telephone the past pastor. This was an attempt to ask for forgiveness. They made several attempts to reach out to the past pastor, but there was never a response. The church members wrote the past pastor a certified letter to express their forgiveness. Although, the past pastor never acknowledged receipt of the letter, it was evident that he had received it. After forgiving the past pastor, the church was able to move ahead. It has grown financially and in membership. The mission of the church extended to the community.

The congregation showed heart forgiveness to the past pastor. Under the leadership of an obedient, godly leader, they were able to move forward. Release was needed in order for the church to grow. We must realize the call of God does not make a person immune from the evils of the world. In this situation, the past pastor was seen as someone who had betrayed the congregation. The congregation took offense to the situation, which caused disunity.

Betrayal is most often followed by offense. There are two reasons people become offended: they have been treated unfairly or they think they have been treated unfairly.

> And they gave the children of Israel a bad report of the land which they had spied out, saying, The land through which we have gone as spies is a land that devours its inhabitants, and all the people whom we saw in it are men of great stature. There we saw the giants; and we were like grasshoppers in our own sight, so we were in their sight. (Numbers 13:32-33)

The children of Israel received the bad report that caused them to turn away from what they believed. We must not allow the things we face to change us. We must be strong enough to always see things from God's prospective. We must remain grounded and rooted in His Word.

Chapter 6

Let It Go

My favorite times of the year are spring and summer. I love the nice crisp air of spring; it is warm and comfortable enough to sit outside and enjoy the wonders of nature. Living on a hill in a rural area makes this a very pleasurable moment. I marvel at God's wonderful creation, extremely amazed at the budding of the trees. I watch the birds as they make haste in preparing for their young.

The grass began to sprout, and the fields were arrayed with multiple colors of wildflowers. I spent countless hours outside. I was not trying to understand the makeup of nature; I was just enjoying God's beautiful creation. As spring drifted into summer, my experience became even more gratifying. The trees were fully clothed in green leaves;

the ground was covered in a layer of green grass. Flowers were in full bloom. People were working outside to enhance God's beauty by adding their own touches to their yards. In the spring, my husband planted his garden; in the summer, he began to enjoy the produce of the garden. I could hear children's voices and laughter and joy sounding across the valley. Over time, the beauty I enjoyed would pass.

I was faced with the realization that my favorite time of the year was coming to an end. During August and September, I spent as much time as possible outside. My heart was sad when the flowers began to wither. The gardens stopped producing. Looking across the hill, I could see the green leaves on the trees changing to many shades of brown. The days were getting shorter. I dreaded the changing of the seasons.

The time outside was my private communication time with God. The time I spent with God as I gazed upon his works was so important. God gave me the title of this chapter in a conversation with coworkers. I was asking God about the contents of this chapter. He reminded me of what I struggled with the most. He reminded me about my struggle with the change of seasons, which led me to Ecclesiastes 3. I learned to embrace whatever season we were in with the understanding that the season I enjoyed most would be back again. When the season returned, it would not be the same as the one that passed. Returning as a renewed season every time, it returned with more to offer. We cannot move into the next season if we are too busy holding on to the things that are passing away in the present season. Why hold onto dead flowers if the garden is no longer producing? In the new season, there will be more pretty flowers. The gardens will produce more than enough.

I had problems letting go of the seasons, and we have problems letting go of other stuff. At some point, we must recognize what we need to let go of. When it is time to let go, we must turn it loose and move on. Our lives are not meant to be lived based on the choices of others. Our lives should be based on what God purposed for us as individuals.

> To every thing there is a season, and a time to every purpose under the heaven: A time to be born, a time to die; a time to plant and a time to pluck up that which is planted. A time to kill, and a time to heal; a time to break down, and a time to build up. A time to weep, and a time to build up. A time to weep, and a time to laugh; a time to morn, and a time to dance. A time to cast away stones, and a time to gather stones together, a time to embrace, and a time to refrain from embracing. A time to get and a time to lose; a time to keep. And a time to cast away. A time to rend, and a time to sew;

a time to keep silence and a time to speak; A time to love, and a time to hate; a time of war, and a time of peace. What profit hath he that worketh in that wherein he laboureth? I have seen the travail which God hath given to the sons of men to be exercised in it. He hath made everything beautiful in his time: also he hath set the world in their heart so that no man can find out the work that God maketh from the beginning to the end. I know that there is no good in them, but for a man to rejoice, and to do good in his life. And also that every man should eat and drink, and enjoy the good of all his labour, it is the gift of God. (Ecclesiastes 3:1-13)

I have read this scripture an uncountable number of times. After seeking God and receiving the directions from God, I went back and read again. The words were the same, but the understanding pierced my heart in a different manner. Not only could I relate this to my inability to accept the change of the season but I could relate it to changes I have experienced in other aspects of my life as well. Being purposed by God, we must understand that change comes with God's purpose. Change means letting go and moving into another position to fulfill God's purpose for our lives. My observance of today's society indicates too many people are living with too much stuff they need to let go. Not understanding the importance of letting go is one of the reasons we hold on to unnecessary stuff. I really enjoyed the summer season and the beauty of nature that came along with it. I didn't want to let go. I would hang on as long as I could—until I realized the beauty of the season had passed away. When the season I really enjoyed passed, I gained a new understanding. The season I enjoyed so much was no longer. I had to accept the fact that this season was over. I must live in the new season and look forward to another spring.

The world is full of changes. Life events can change the direction of life and the conditions of life. God showed me that changes come into our lives for a reason. Changes are necessary for spiritual growth and human development. Change is ordained by God, put in place by God, and determined by God. Take a look at the horizon. The clouds and the earth appear to come together. Although the clouds and the earth are separate, they appear to flow as one. It is an evolving circle. Although they appear to be one, the clouds give way to the beginning of earth, and earth gives way to the beginning of the clouds. Night and day are two different times, but each takes its turn to come into play. We learn to allow the seasons of our lives to flow from one to the next. We accept change that opens the door for growth.

A balanced life is fulfilled by the perseverance of the mind that expects change. The world changes daily, and we must never expect tomorrow to be the same as today. Although today may be cloudy, expect the sun to shine tomorrow. The sun cannot hide behind the clouds forever. Just as a person cannot be held forever in captivity by fear, unforgiveness, abuse, rejection, and addictions, change must come. Some changes are acts of God—and some depend on the will of man—but all are determined by divine purpose. As long as we live in our human forms, we can expect change. When we transition into our spiritual lives and move to our permanent homes, there will be no more change.

Whatever the season may be, we are called to live in that season. Living in the present season gives us what we need to live in the next season. When we were children, our parents taught us about life as we progressed through the many stages of life. Parents nurture their children from one stage of life to another. Every stage of life was a season we had to move through. There were times we felt we knew more about the season we were in than our parents did. This is the same thing we do as adults; instead of allowing God to hold our hands through the seasons, we try to travel without him. There is no way people can progress through the seasons that come into our lives without the overseer of the seasons.

Ecclesiastes 1:1-13 tells us of the various seasons we have to endure on this earth. The first season it speaks of is the season of being born and dying. The scripture tells us there is a time to be born and a time to die. It does not say there is a time to be born, a time to live, and a time to die. The time to be born and the time to die is set by divine order. When we were born, we immediately began the dying process. Every breath we take is one less breath we have left, which moves us closer to death. Life in between birth and death is short. How we choose to live our short lives is up to us. Our lives are purposed; do we live it by fulfilling the purpose or living useless lives filled with stuff?

The second verse tells us there are times to plant and times to pluck. In the spring, my husband plants a garden that will produce food in the summer. The garden yields food for a given time. After the time for producing is over, the plants wither. They do not completely go away. In order to be able to plant again in this area, my husband has to pluck up the withered plants. Removing the withered plants allows the ground to be prepared for the next season. After a while, the spot where the garden is planted becomes barren. The garden has to be moved to another location. In the ministry, we plant seeds. As long as good fruit is being produced from the planting, all is good. When the seeds are not producing, it's time to pluck up the barren fruit trees and move your garden to a new location.

There are times to weep and times to laugh. There are times to mourn and times to dance. These go hand and hand. There are many reasons why we weep; when the weeping passes, there is time to laugh. There are times to mourn about the ways of the world and times to dance. Rejoice in God for what he has done and will do for the land. We were created to praise and worship God, and he expects us to serve him with joyful hearts. Weeping and mourning are positioned first in the statement. This allows us to know that it is okay to shed tears and be mournful. The tears and sorrow move us to a place of communion with Jesus, which brings us joy. We weep in times of sorrow. We weep when hard times cause us to be confused. We weep when our loved ones are hurt. We weep when life's circumstances change for what we believe to be the worst. After the weeping, joy comes. We see the changes and understand they are for the better. Weeping may last for a night, but joy comes in the morning. Praise God from whom all blessings flow!

There is a time to cast away stones and a time to gather stones. There comes a time when we must tear down the stones that have been put in place as protection. Stones are piled high when there is no peace in one's heart. At some point, we must tear down the walls, placing our trust in God and realizing He is our protector. Let go of whatever in your heart is holding those stone together. The wall has to be rebuilt when others try to invade our lives. If the stones are rebuilt, it is only for a season before the time comes to tear them down again.

There are times to embrace and times to refrain from embracing. We all have someone in our lives who we believed was a true friend. We trusted the person with our most valuable possessions. In the end, this person was not a friend. They have done everything to undermine you in every possible way. They have talked about you to other friends, misled you, and set you up for failure. Although you have embraced this person, when the truth is revealed, it is time to refrain from embracing. There comes a time when you must keep a distance from this person. A friend is not unjust, unfaithful, or unfair. In some situations, refraining from embracing may not be enough. It may be time to let them go. You have the responsibility to forgive and move on.

> Defraud ye not one the other, except it be with consent for a time, that ye may give yourselves to fasting and prayer; and to come together again, that Satan tempt you not for your incontinency. (I Corinthians 7:5)

There is a time to get and a time to lose—a time to keep and a time to cast away. There is a time in life when the getting is good. We get money and great opportunities, and we are able to seek and get things of this world. It might be a great job, a beautiful home, or a pretty sports car. There is a time for getting busy and maintaining the things of this world. There is also a time to get wisdom, knowledge, and experience.

Just as there is a time to get, there is a time to lose. The monetary gain from hard work at a great job is no longer for a reason; it's all about change getting and losing, keeping and letting go. Just as the night rolls into day and the day into night, the same thing takes place in attaining and losing, keeping and letting go. All of you have attained something you didn't want to let go of. I remember receiving a wonderful Christmas gift from my daughter and son-in-law. It was a beautiful diamond cross necklace with a special designer chain. It was not an overbearing piece of jewelry; it was beautiful and modest. I was blessed to be given such a prized item. I vowed to keep the necklace for a lifetime; it meant so much to me. Even though the necklace was given to me as a gift, I was able to get it. I enjoyed it and cherished it and only wore it occasionally.

One Sunday, I wore the necklace, but when I returned home, I did not remove the necklace. I ran several errands that day. At some point, I felt for the necklace—and it was not there. I had lost the necklace. I didn't know how it happened or where I lost it. I was so sad about the necklace when I realized it was lost. Nothing more could be done. There was a good side to this event. I tried to find one just like it, but I was unsuccessful. My husband gave me another necklace for my birthday, which I now cherish. We must realize that when we get and lose things, there are times we lose to gain something we could not get until we lost something else. For example, people may feel they cannot live without their good jobs. One day, they are laid off. Months later, after many applications, the old job has been replaced with a better job. I used an example of a material item, but getting and losing can relate to all aspects of your life. One may get understanding and lose the wisdom that came with that understanding. You may get a dear friend and think you will be friends forever. When circumstances cause you to lose that friend—no matter what you get or lose—it's all for a reason. You may never understand why. No one can hold onto something or someone who is no longer there.

Also, there is a time to keep and a time to let go. Keeping and letting go is all about knowing when to let go and what to let go of. My examples have been about items, but I pray that they also open the door for understanding in all aspects of life. We all try to hang onto things we don't need anymore or things that no longer serve purposes in our lives. The most practical example that comes to mind is clothes. We all have clothes hanging in our closets that are no longer serving a purpose for us. Although they serve no purpose for us, they can be useful to someone else. This mean it is time to let go. Our closets are filled with clothes we purchased and didn't like after we got them home. We purchased clothes that were a size too small and rationalized the purchases by saying we will lose weight. Some clothes are out of style, and some we have outgrown. We keep the clothing by fooling ourselves about the future and the use of the clothes at a later date. Clothes hang in our closets for years, serving no purpose for us. There comes a time when we must face the facts and release the items from our possession. If we let go of the clothes, we can bless someone who doesn't have anything to wear.

There are many things we need to let go that no longer serve a purpose to us. There are people in our lives we need to let go of and spiritual strongholds we need to let go of. There are two types of people we cross in our lifetimes. There are those who support us and encourage us to live our visions, which enhances our growth. There are those who are always giving us negative feedback and talking down our visions.

The people who stick with you through the good times and the worst times are the ones to keep in your life. They act as a cheering team when you want to give up. They may not see your vision, but they can join you in fulfilling the vision God has given you.

They understand who you are. There comes a time to let go of anyone in your life who is filled with negativity. They are anxious to tear you down or set you up for failure.

They cause confusion and enjoy seeing others fail. They speak untruths in order to bring others against you. It's hard letting go of family members. We have a preconceived idea that family members will be our supporters when no one else will. The truth is that in some cases, family members are your worst enemies. We must know who we need to let go of—and let God handle our evildoers.

In our spiritual walk, there comes a time when we must let go of rituals and traditions in order to move to the next level. Christians go through the actions of living as Christians but hinder their growth by not really knowing the true meaning of what is expected of believers.

One example of worshipping rituals is the act of Holy Communion. Now, don't misunderstand me. I regard the administering of Holy Communion as a very sacred act, but in some cases, we have forgotten what it represents. We have gotten hung up on the act itself, forgetting the one it represents. Churches are becoming more concerned with increasing memberships and offerings. They have forgotten to focus. The church was built for reaching lost souls. Christians in this weary world have peace on earth only through Jesus Christ when we rest in him. Toiling for Jesus is to labor in a sorrowful land. We can rest when we get home. Every change we endure prepares us for the upcoming changes.

My grandmother lived to be 106. Until her death on June 28, 2011, she was in her right mind. She often spoke about the changes she had witnessed in her lifetime. She said, "I have seen changes—some good, some bad. I haven't always agreed with or understood the changes, but change must come."

Can you imagine the changes she saw in her lifetime and how they must have affected her? My grandmother was a woman of God. She thanked God for allowing her to live such a long life. She said, "Changes are what they are—all based on God's will."

She helped me understand that whatever life has for us, we must make the best of it. We must believe it is best for the present. Everything is as God has made it. Everything that comes into our lives—and the timing—has been appointed by God. We must be pleased and trust God through the changes that come into our lives. We must accept with glad hearts that it is the will of God. Let go of the stuff we don't need, embrace change, and know the darkness of night evolves into the light of day.

Chapter 7
Do Not Be Deceived

Fearing change is the deception of the enemy who is trying to distract you from your purpose. Allowing yourself to be deceived by the enemy places a barrier between you and God. Not being able to see God through Jesus Christ sets you up for failure.

> Then Haman said to King Ahasuerus, "There is a certain people scattered and dispersed among the people in all the provinces of your kingdom; their laws are different from all other peoples, and they do not keep the king's laws. Therefore it is not fitting for the king to let them remain. If it pleases the king, let a decree be written that they be destroyed, and I will pay ten thousand

> talents of silver into the hands of those who do
> the work, to bring it unto the king's treasuries.
> (Esther 3:8-9)

Haman gave an evil report to the king with the object of distracting him. There are times when an evil report may be true but given with the wrong motive. Haman desired to convince the king that some among them were not willing to obey the laws. He tried to create disunity and division among the people—violating the king's spirit by secretly planning to betray him. The report distorted the truth, which influenced the king and caused him to form an evil opinion.

To be deceived means walking in a spirit of confusion. When we enter a state of confusion, we listen to conflicting stories that will not allow us to submit to God for guidance.

It causes us to lose sight of what is really important for our purpose. "In thee, O Lord, do I put my trust; let me never be put in confusion" (Psalm 71:1).

Deception impacts every facet of our lives as well as those around us. Deception creates disorder, which is motivated by other underlying reasons. Deception by causing confusion prevents us from seeing the source of the issues because of what has been implanted in our spirits. Deception causes confusion, which is a defilement of the righteous spirit. There is no way anyone can accept change by walking in a state of confusion brought on by deception. When someone has been deceived, the state of confusion causes anger, bitterness, mockery, envy, selfishness, guilt, and pride—things Christians are warned not to walk in. Deception by way of evil or false reports has destroyed families, undermined the authority in God's churches, and separated families. This defiles the name of Jesus and makes the Holy Spirit grieve. When there are misunderstandings in families, it is important to come together for understanding. One false report can destroy the lives of many, accomplishing its purpose, which is to divide and conquer.

We cannot allow our spirits to be contaminated with the uncleanness and ungodliness of deception. "The north wind driveth away the rain; so doth an angry countenance. A backbiting tongue" (Proverbs 25:23).

Contamination of the spirit can occur anywhere—in a godly place or an ungodly place. In the midst of an ungodly place, you can hold on to your godliness. God has given us the gift of discernment. Through this holy gift, we have the ability to discern between good and bad. We see the thoughts and the intent of the heart. We discern between righteousness and wickedness. God has instilled in us wisdom to give way to peace and mercy and good fruit. Proverbs 16:16 tells us that wisdom is more precious than gold.

God requires us to attain knowledge of His Word. Knowledge gives us what we need to see from a spiritual aspect. With knowledge, we can prevail in God's grace. With knowledge, we are able to conduct ourselves in a godly manner. The revelation of God's Word brings us profitable results and makes us able to receive understanding. We prevail through wisdom, knowledge, and revelation.

Accept change—but don't allow yourself to get caught up in the works of backbiters. They speak against people in their absence. Don't be deceived by the busybody who searches for information by means of gossip, slander, and backbiting. Don't take time to listen to a complainer who finds fault in everything or everyone. Stay away from the murmurer who grumbles about everything and never sees the good in anything. Be mindful of those who slander or try to injure reputations by sharing damaging situations or stories. Don't be deceived into believing that listening to false reports is okay. Listening to a false report from another person means you identify with the one bringing the report. To identify with someone means to emotionally, intellectually, or spiritually connect.

Stop and think before you allow yourself to be sucked into identifying with someone you don't really connect with. If you don't plan to have to explain that you were just listening, there are some ways to combat a person who brings evil reports. Ask yourself and the person bringing the repost if it is something you need to hear. "The heart of the prudent acquires knowledge and the ear of the wise seeks knowledge" (Proverbs 18:15).

What part of the conversation needs to be discussed with me? I am going to take notes so I can recall the details. Do you mind?

"The grumbles, complainers, walking according to their own lusts; And they mouth great swelling words, flattering people to gain advantage" (Jude 16).

Who told you this information? Is this your interpretation of what you heard—or did you actually observe the incident? Is it okay if I quote you when I check this out? In telling me this, what are you expecting me to do? How do you feel about this situation? Have you spoken to the people involved? Is it okay that I don't respond until I pray about the information? Asking these questions will cause the person bringing the report to think twice before sharing.

> Moreover if your brother sins against you, go and tell him his fault between you and him alone. If he hears you, you have gained your brother. (Matthew 18:15)

> Brethren, if a man is overtaken in any trespass, you who are spiritual restore such a one in a

spirit of gentleness, considering Yourself lest

you also be tempted. (Galatians 6:1-2)

Once people have been deceived and deception has won their spirits, the enemy takes over their lives. They are misled by false reports and refuse to listen, investigate, or receive the truth. After being overtaken by the spirit of deception, the individual received another's offense and used it as an excuse for rebellion. They go from place to place, seeking out false or evil reports about people. A person overtaken by deception does not like acting alone; they seek out others to agree with them. They are tricked into believing they are doing the will of God by rebelling against another person. They refuse to seek or receive help because they truly believe everyone else is wrong. They also isolate themselves from godly contacts with anyone seeking to reach out to them.

We should not allow ourselves to be caught up into being deceived by others. We all are held accountable for what we do and how we handle life's changes. Life changes can be brought on naturally or induced by others. We allow ourselves to get caught up in the things of this world. They play on our minds, leading us down the road of destruction. In Romans, Paul addressed an issue I had to think hard about. Paul revealed several parallels between chapter 6 and 7. In chapter 6, Paul uses the word *sin* seventeen times. In chapter 7, he used the word *law* nineteen times. It was revealed to me that the statement used in Romans 6:14 has confused many believers. "For sin shall not be master over you, for you are not under the law, but under grace."

Many believe since we are no longer under the law, we do not have to live by the laws. The laws are the commandments given by God. After God sent His Son Jesus Christ to die for our sins, his blood covered us. But that does not excuse us from keeping God's commandments and following His laws. In the beginning, people were taught the law. After the death of Jesus, the law should be in the heart of man.

Living as God commanded and living under the grace of God go hand in hand. We are deceived into believing that we can change the laws of God based on what people decide is right or wrong. We should not allow our morals as believers to be compromised in any way. Write the laws of God in your heart—and live each day knowing the blood of Jesus covers us.

Believers have a duty to honor and respect. We have to honor and respect that we have victory over sin, but it's only by way of Jesus Christ, his death, and resurrection. Paul stated in Romans 7 the law was given to arouse the sinful nature in us. In other words, the law is good, but human nature is the problem. When we do not obey the law, we sin. For example, on the highway, the speed limit is sixty miles per hour. There are consequences if the speed limit is exceeded. In spite of the law, some drivers go faster, which is contrary to the law.

The speeding driver is as a believer who knows the law of God. The law tells us we are not to commit adultery. The sinful nature is aroused, and God is dishonored.

Before Jesus came, we were under the law. Once he came and died for our sins, we were justified by the shedding of his blood. We should know the law but not live the law because living the law incites sin in the newness of the Holy Spirit. Knowing this, I remind you that it is important to strive daily for perfection, knowing we are saved by grace as we maintain our morals.

> And he said unto him. Why callest thou me good? There is none good but one that is God: but if thou will enter into life: keep the commandments. (Matthew 19:17)

> Because the law worketh wrath: for where no law is, there is no transgression. (Romans 4:16)

If you never see a sign that says keep off the grass, you are never tempted to walk on the grass. Once you see the sign over and over again, human nature is aroused—and you desire to walk on the grass. The law does not quench the desire to sin, but the love of God should give us the desire to strive to do the right things.

Everyone is accountable for his or her choices. The laws should be written on the tablets in our hearts. We are covered by the grace of God by way of His Son Jesus. Knowing the laws and understanding the grace of God, we should desire to live as Jesus did on earth. Many believe accepting Jesus in our lives is sufficient. This is merely the beginning. There is so much more, and we must show and live it. We allow ourselves to become relaxed in the way we live, believing that going through the motions is good enough. We must be willing to give God our best at all times. When it comes to doing the work of God, we shy away from anything that inconvenience us. We are called to live in the world, but we are not apart from the world. So many believers live lives that dishonor God. If church lasts over one hour, we choose to stay home. If being a member of a ministry entails using your free time, you refuse to participate. We have taken our eyes off God and put them on ourselves. Our actions—the things we do and say—must always be in agreement with God's Word.

> For if the firstfruit be holy, the lump is also holy:
> and if the root be Holy, so are the branches.
> (Romans 11:16)

I encourage every believer to work on his or her relationship with God. Don't just go through the ritual of being a believer. Walk the walk and let the light of God shine through you. Don't be guilty of worshipping rituals. Honor the rituals for what they stand for. Worship God—the only one deserving of this honor. Give God the glory and honor only He deserves!

Chapter 8
Worship in Spirit and Truth

Who shall separate us from the Love of Christ? Shall trouble
or hardship or persecution or famine or nakedness or danger or
Sword? As it is written: "For your sake we face death all day long
we are considered as sheep to be slaughtered." No, in all these
things we are more than conquerors through him who loved us.
For I am convinced that neither death nor life, neither angels nor
demons, neither the present nor the future, not any powers, neither
height nor depth, nor anything else in all creation will be able to
separate us from the love of God that is in Christ Jesus our Lord.

—Romans 8:35-39

In the past chapters, I discussed the seasons of life. In
every season, there is a purpose for that season in your life.
The harder the season we pass through, the stronger our

relationship with God. The harder the season, the harder
we pray. The harder the season, the more determined we
become. We become our weakest in some seasons, and we
become stronger when we come out of the season. In the
midst of our hardest season, God is there. We must place
our trust in Him. Your days may be as dark as night right
now. You may be fighting what you consider a losing battle.
Disappointments may be coming at you from all directions.
This is a season to cast all your cares upon God through
prayer. Give God your burdens. He will see you through this
season. In this season, God is reminding you of who He is
and whose you are. If you are in your day season, God still
wants you to give Him the honor and glory for the season
He has brought you through.

> I sought the Lord and he answered me; He
> delivered me from all my fears. Those who look
> to him are radiant; their faces are never covered
> with shame. This poor man called, and the
> Lord heard him; He save him out of all his
> troubles. The angel of the Lord heard him; He
> saved him out of all his troubles. The angel of
> the Lord encamps around those who fear him,
> and he delivers them. Taste and see the Lord is
> good: Blessed is the man who takes refuge in
> him. (Psalm 34:4-8)

There is nothing more important to me than my meditation time. I look forward to uninterrupted time with God early in the morning. There are times when my meditation time is cut short because of life events. There are times when I start, stop, and restart my meditations.

I would love to spend some intimate time with God—with no interruptions. I would love to give Him the glory and honor for all things. We are called worship God in spirit and truth. What exactly does that mean? The purpose of our worship is to glorify, honor, praise, lift up God, and please Him. We are to be appreciative for Him providing us an escape from the stronghold of sin. As a child, I often heard that salvation is free. But it is by way of worship that we receive salvation. God wants us to worship Him with our mouths, hearts, and souls. True worship is humbling and submitting yourself before God. Worshipping is a humbling action that gives reverence to the one true God.

> God resists the proud, but gives grace to the humble. Humble yourselves in the sight of the Lord, and He will lift you up. (James 4:6, 10)

How can anyone sit quietly during worship service and not show any emotions? True worship is not based on emotional reactions. Emotions are the basis for how we react in situations. For example, the choir may sing a song that bring back memories and cause you to become emotional.

Emotionally reacting is based on what you are feeling about something. There are times I hear a song my mother used to sing. Hearing the song, I began to weep. I am feeling emotions about the song and expressing it through my actions. Sitting quietly as you worship God does not mean your worship is not real. Are you worshipping from your soul? Is God your only focus? Are you in a humble state? The only conditions placed on worship are that we must worship in spirit and truth. The word *must* is defined as an obligation, a requirement, or something done because it is a necessity.

God knows my heart. Since God knows our hearts, we need to be sure our worship is real. God seeks out the true worshippers; I long for nothing more than to be sought by God. I want to be identified as one who worships in spirit and truth. I do not have a desire to please others by the way I worship. I only want to please God by worshipping in spirit and truth. My soul is my only concern. God is the object of my worship—not people. God alone deserves to be worshipped. He decides how we are to worship. We look to God for guidance, and we must worship the way He requires us to. "O Lord, I know that the way of man is not in himself, it is not in man who walks to direct his own steps" (Jeremiah 10:23).

When we worship, we must keep several things in mind. Worshipping is personal time with God. During this time, we must be sincere and show love and respect to our Creator.

> God who made the world and everything in it, since He is Lord of heaven and earth, does not dwell in temples made with hands, as through He needed anything since He gives life, breath, and all things. (Acts 17:24-25)

God holds our destinies in His hands. We understand that salvation is free but worship secures our salvation. Worship in spirit and truth now because Judgment Day will be too late. "Work out your own salvation with fear and trembling" (Philippians 2:12).

In worship, we realize just how unworthy we are. God reigns above all others. God don't need our worship, but we are required to worship to please Him. Worship brings us closer to God and strengthens our relationship with Him. "Draw near to God and He will draw near to you" (James 4:8).

We should worship God to please Him and for our own strength. It strengthens us and aids in the developing of the character of Christ. "Let this mind be in you which was also in Christ" (Philippians 2:5).

Drawing close to God is a constant renewing of the mind. "And do not be conformed to this world, but be transformed by renewing of your mind" (Romans 12:2).

We need to constantly worship God in and out of seasons. Sincere worship gets us through good and bad times. Through worship, we develop the important traits that ensure we will not be deceived by evildoers. We are able to walk in forgiveness, righteousness, kindness, love, and many more of the traits that prepare us for eternal life. "Set your mind on thing above, and not on things on the earth" (Colossians 3:2).

God is to be worshipped in spirit and truth. God directs our ways as believers. God is the giver of life, and it is He we are to worship. We are to work out our salvation with fear and trembling. We are to seek Christlike characteristics as we draw near to God. In all things, we are not to be changed by the ways of the world. We are changed by renewing the mind. It does not matter the manner in which we worship our Lord and Savior, but it must be done in spirit and truth. Worship is not the songs the choir sings. It is not the amount of money you can place in the collection basket. Worship is not about how many ministries you become a member of. These are only acts of expression of worship. These acts in no way define what true worship really is. We are not to get caught up in worship that only acknowledges God's blessings in our lives. Worship God because He is sovereign and deserves to be worshipped.

God responds to us through worship because he chooses to. It is promised that when we worship God, He will commune with us. In worship, the heavy loads we bear are lightened. Worship is the mending of a broken spirit, which is the key to completeness in Christ. Worship in spirit and truth is one receiving nothing but giving everything.

> Give and it will be given to you; good measure, pressed down, shaken together, and running over will be pour into your bosom. For the measure that you use, it will measured back to you. (Luke 6:38)

In worship, we cannot continue to attend church and expect the worship service to deposit into your spirit. To get something out of worship service we must put something in. Many associate Luke 6:38 with financial blessings. I see it as a guideline for worship. If you worship God in spirit, truth, and good measure, God will receive your worship. He is able to receive more of your worship. When something is shaken, it is mixed well, which pleases God. God is so pleased with your worship that He opens His door of generosity and pours out many blessings. If you don't give, you don't receive.

The mood of a worshipper is based on the attitude of the heart. The heart can be excited in worship, just like

Miriam and the women of Israel after their deliverance from Egypt. David worshipped God with a different attitude; he worshipped God following the death of his baby boy. Although the tone was different, both were considered to be worship in spirit and truth. I have not read anything in the Bible that says our worship has to be some type of strange encounter that no one understand. Worshipping comes from deep within oneself, combining the mind, will, and emotions in a Christlike spirit.

When you hear people say they go to church but they get nothing out of the worship service, it's not the worship service that needs reforming—it's the worshipper. Churches can spend a lot of time trying to adjust the service. Changing or improving the form has nothing to do with correcting the hearts of those who come to worship. I pray that God will lead you to that place of worship in spirit and truth.

We need to let go of the unnecessary stuff in our lives and worship God in spirit and truth. Communion with God through Jesus Christ removes the junk from our lives. Ask God to cleanse you from whatever is contaminating your body. Pray your way through your seasons. Pray for constant cleansing of your thoughts and mind. Speak the truth, and your enemies will flee from you. Examine your motives in life to make sure you are walking in forgiveness.

Chapter 9

Come to the Feast

We have all been invited to a great feast. It is time to pick up your invitation and come to the feast. What is this great feast? Is it the great feast? It is the Supper of the Lamb. We have been invited to sit at the Lord's table to sup with Him. My mind goes back to the man who attended the king's wedding celebration but was not dressed for the occasion.

God is standing at the head of the table with His hands outstretched, saying, "Come. I gave you My word to study so that you may prepare yourself for this great celebration."

Are you dressed for the occasion? Jesus gave His life so that we may have a place at His table. He gave so much and required so little of us.

Our invitation is to a greater celebration than we could ever know on earth. It is the wedding of the Lamb when Jesus comes back to take his bride (the church). This church has no spots or wrinkles. Preparing for this celebration is of the utmost importance. Most places of worship set aside times to look back and remember what Jesus did for us when He died on the cross. We take the time to look back, and we look forward to the great celebration.

The man who attended the wedding celebration for the king's son in Matthew 22:8-10 was not dressed for the occasion. He had not taken all the necessary steps to prepare himself for the celebration. He walked into the king's mansion like a muddy mess, covered in worldly sludge. Paul in his letter to the Church of Corinth cautioned us against attending the feast not dressed for the occasion. We must pay close attention to the instructions of Paul in preparing for the great feast.

> Wherefore whosoever shall eat this bread and drink this cup unworthily, shall be guilty of the body and blood of the Lord. But let a man examine himself, and so let him eat of that bread and drink of that cup. For he that eateth and drinketh unworthily eateth and drinketh damnation to himself, not discerning the Lord's body. For this cause many are weak and sickly

among you and many sleep. For if we would judge ourselves, we should not be judged. (1 Corinthians 11:27-31)

Paul is saying that we must be prepared. Take a close look at ourselves to ensure that we are dressed for the occasion. What must you wear to the great celebration: a spirit that worships in spirit and truth? A right relationship with God through Jesus Christ? To lack a spirit of worship and a relationship with the Father means you are not dressed for the occasion. There is no cost to attend, but we are required to be worthy of being in the presence of God. We must take the invitation of God to the wedding celebration of His Son very seriously.

I have been in the congregations of many churches when they remembered what Jesus did for us by partaking in the practice of Holy Communion. This ritual needs to be honored for what it represents. The act represents the death of Christ, and we treat it as such by being worthy of partaking. The man at the king's wedding was bound and cast into darkness.

We are told there will be weeping and gnashing of teeth. Weeping and gnashing of teeth lets us know that the place where anyone unworthy will go will not be heaven. In heaven, all our tears will be wiped away. There will be no more crying and no more pain. I encourage you to get dressed, stay dressed, and treat every day as if the great celebration has started. Stop looking at others and pointing out the wrong in them. Examine yourself so that you are worthy of attending.

Are you a true believer and a humble child of God? If you are, you have the right to go to the feast with your invitation in hand. If you are not—and you are not willing to prepare for the feast—you might as well throw your invitation in the trash.

As a child, I attended church every Sunday and participated in many youth functions. The fourth Sunday of each month stands out in my mind. At 2:30, the Lord's Supper was administered. On the other Sundays, services were held at 11:30. The women would be dressed in white, and the men wore black suits and white shirts. The pastor would be dressed in a black suit and white shirt. Much effort was put into making this service special. The elders of the church would say, "This is communion Sunday. You need to be on your best behavior."

A special table was stationed at the front of the church. Sometimes the children would unintentionally lean on or touch the table. The adults would come from everywhere to scold us for the mistake. The sacred table was not touched unless it was the fourth Sunday during Holy Communion. When the Holy Communion was administered, we were not allowed to move about or talk to anyone. Chewing gum was not allowed. It was a time to remember Jesus Christ dying for us on the Cross. I often think back when I see the Lord's Supper being administered. There are people checking their cell phones and children playing. Today, the ritual of the Lord's Supper is being treated as a casual occurrence. As a child, I was taught to honor the tradition of Holy Communion. As an adult, I understand the honor of partaking in this ritual.

Accepting God's invitation to the great celebration affords us the opportunity to sit with His Son as we break bread together. The ritual of administering the Lord's Supper, as with the body of Christ, should be as if we were already in the presence of the Lord. The Lord's Supper is a time to focus on the fact that our Lord, Jesus Christ, died so that we could attend. When we partake in the act of Holy Communion, we should equate it to the meal Jesus shared with His Apostles. He said, "Do this in remembrance of me."

Jesus commissioned the Apostles and gave them the authority to celebrate Holy Communion the same as He had done. The act of Holy Communion represents the broken body of Jesus and the forgiveness by the shedding of Jesus's blood. When we partake of the bread, we acknowledge what Jesus did for us and look forward to His return. Hebrews 4:16 tell us that Jesus's blood gives us the right standing before God, allowing us to go boldly into God's presence. God hears our prayers.

Paul told us to examine ourselves before eating and drinking at the Lord's table. Partaking in an unworthy manner brings judgment. The key to fully experiencing the full meaning of being a partaker in the Lord's Supper starts with humbling yourself.

> God resists the proud but gives grace to the humble. Humble yourselves therefore under the mighty hand of God so that He may exalt you in due time. (1 Peter 5:5-6)

On the night of the Last Supper, Jesus knew His death was near. He did not dwell on His death; he spent the time giving instructions to the disciples. The disciples chose to focus on who was considered the greatest among them. The greatest in Jesus's sight are the ones who humble themselves as servants. We often spend time seeking greatness, which gains nothing in the kingdom of God.

Jesus led by example. He showed the disciples what being a servant meant. He didn't focus on himself. Jesus took a towel and basin of water and washed the feet of the disciples. As he washed their feet he said. "You call me Teacher and Lord. This is well said, for I am. So if I, your Lord and Teacher, have washed your feet, you also ought to wash one another's feet. For I have given you an example that you also should do just as I have done for you" (John 13:13-15).

Just as the disciples were divided on the eve of the Last Supper, many churches today are divided. Talk about confused! Jesus was in the room with the disciples, and they were arguing over who would be the greatest. Jesus is in the church today, but we can't see Him because we are busy arguing over who is the greatest. Pastors, leaders, and lay leaders are divided, causing turmoil in the congregation. Members are leaving the church over foolishness. The church family shows very little love for each other. There is no humility among us.

Pride and sin go hand in hand. Pride causes us to be arrogant, which causes us to become disoriented and forget our missions. Strong pride can lead to sin and cause others to sin. The spirit of pride goes hand in hand with everything Jesus is not. Pride bred a spirit of disobedience, self-exaltation, faultfinding, gossiping, impatience, a critical spirit, boastfulness, complaining, and demanding, rude, and selfish motives. When self is involved, there is no God involved.

Pride drives us to chase after our own evil desires and walk in a judgmental spirit and sexual immorality. It is as if we have been issued a license to sin. My heart grieves that so many Christians walk in this spirit and forget their first love. It's time to let go of everything and anyone who is hindering your spiritual growth. Let go. Take your eyes off of other people and look only to our Creator. Just think about the things we sometimes face—the opposition and humiliation we don't understand. We call it spiritual warfare, but this may be God's work. We often blame the devil for the things we go through when it can be God's work because of the spirit of pride His children walk in.

> O love the Lord, all ye his saints: for the Lord preserveth the faithful, and plentifully rewardeth the proud doer. (Psalm 31:23)

> The fear of the Lord is to hate evil: pride, and arrogancy, and the evil way, and the forward mouth, do I hate. (Proverbs 8:13)

> Every one that is proud in heart is an abomination to the Lord: though hand join in hand, he shall not be unpunished. (Proverbs 16:5)

> Likewise, ye younger, submit yourselves unto the elder. Yea, all of you be subject one to another, and be clothed with humility: for God Resisteth the Proud, and Giveth grace to the Humble. Humble yourselves therefore under the mighty hand of God, that he may exalt you in due time. (1 Peter 5:5-6)

When you humble yourself before God, you give Him the glory He deserves through your life.

Know without a doubt that God will lift you up in due time. You may be asking two questions. *Am I guilty of being arrogant? How can I humble myself?* The thing about pride is that it keeps us quiet and restricts us from openly admitting things we should. Therefore, dealing with the sin of pride, we must openly admit the spirit of pride exists within us. Not openly admitting the sin of pride to God and others strengthens the spirit of pride. We can be humbled by developing the Christlike spirit within us. If we choose not to humble ourselves, God will humiliate us to teach us humility. My studies revealed some actions we need to take in humbling ourselves.

- Always acknowledge God's sovereignty.
- Agree with God about your sin and repent of the sin.
- Give God the glory for all things in your life.
- Accept lowly tasks without complaining.
- Submit to those in authority over you without complaining.
- Serve others.
- Set aside your plans, opinions, and desires for those of others.
- When leading, lead from a position of loving service to those you lead.

- Openly confess sin when it is appropriate.
- Admit to your weakness or needs and ask for help when needed.
- Be willing to socialize with people you feel are lower than you.
- Give to the needy.
- Don't be ashamed to ask for prayer.
- Allow others to do for you.
- Know that it is only through Christ that you can do all things.
- Never put yourself above others.
- Put the desires or wishes of others ahead of yours.
- Don't do things for others to be well spoken of.
- Give yourself over to God—let Him guide your every decision.

Developing a spirit of humility is needed if you plan to accept your invitation to the wedding supper of the Lamb.

God wants us to accept the invitation He has extended. When our actions are contrary to His Word, He doesn't give up on us. God has given us much power; this power comes by way of choice. We can choose to live for Him, love Him, and follow Him. We have the choice to attend the great celebration. God is saying, "Come to the Feast." Will you be dressed for the occasion—or will you be bound and cast into darkness? Because Jesus died for us, we are no longer slaves to sin. We can choose to be a slave of God by walking in righteousness. God adopted us into His royal family. It's time we live as true members of His family. God never gives up on us. He works daily to mold us to be like His Son. We need to accept His invitation and conform to the likeness of Jesus. Because God is gentle, loving, and kind, we should thirst after Him for who He is. Do you have a sincere desire to be like Him? Are you willing to do His will?

Whatever It Takes
L. W. Wolfe

There's a voice calling me from an old rugged tree,
And it whispers,
"Draw closer to Me;
Leave this world far behind, there are new heights
To climb.
And a new place in Me you will find."
For whatever it takes to draw closer to You, Lord,
That's what I'll be willing to do; For whatever it takes
To be more like You.
That's what I'll be willing to do.
Take the dearest things to me, if that's how it must be
To draw me closer to You;
Let the disappointments come, lonely days without the sun,

If through sorrow more like You I'll become.

Take my houses and lands, change my dreams and my plans,

For I am placing my whole life in Your hands;

And if you call me today to a land far away, Lord I'll go and Your will obey.

I'll trade sunshine for rain, comfort for pain, that's what I'll Be willing to do;

For whatever it takes for my will be break, that's what I'll Be willing to do.

You don't have to be perfect to accept the invitation, but you must be willing to strive for perfection. Our brokenness is revealed to us to that we may be healed and not condemned. Jesus knows all about us. He knows our weaknesses, our hearts, and our needs. Jesus did not condemn the woman caught in the act of adultery. He told her to go and not sin anymore (John 8:11). When we put on the character of Christ, we are dressed in His salvation and ready to attend the feast. Let go of the foolishness. Let go of the things you don't need in your life. Get dressed for the occasion. Come to the feast—and you will not hunger or thirst anymore. The Lord is waiting at the table to welcome you with open arms. Come to the Lord's table and receive rest for your weary soul.

As you prepare to sit at the Lord's table, open your mind and heart to receive all that God has for you at the table of His Son. Cry out God as you enter His presence. Go to the table to worship Him in spirit and in truth. Surrender yourself to Him so that you may be renewed and strengthened to overcome the things of this world. Pray for an overflow of the Holy Spirit to overcome the desires of the flesh. Thank Him for all things and for the changes He is able to bring about in your life. We are connected to Jesus by the shedding of His blood. What a blessing it is to be one in attendance at the great feast. Sit at the table with Jesus because He loves you so much. Come to the feast!

I have a passion for hymns. When I think of salvation, a song by Fanny Crosby comes to mind. Crosby wrote the tune but had no words. She carried the tune to Phoebe Palmer Knapp. When she heard the music, God gave her the words. The song represents assurance, submission, prize, and salvation. Many people consider this song a favorite.

It was a favorite of my father. As a child, I heard him sing it as he worked around the house. I relate to this song in the same way my father did. I am so glad I have the blessed assurance of knowing that Jesus is mine.

Blessed Assurance
Fanny Crosby

Blessed assurance, Jesus is mine!

O what a foretaste of glory divine!

Heir of salvation, purchase of God,

Born of His Spirit, washed in His blood.

This is my story, this is my song,

Praising my Savior all the day long;

This is my story, this is my song,

Praising my Savior all the day long.

Perfect submission, perfect delight!

Visions of rapture now burst on my sight;

Angels descending bring from above

Echoes of mercy, whispers of love.

Perfect submission—all is at rest,

I in my Savior am happy and blest;

Watching and waiting, looking above,

Filled with His goodness, lost in His love.

Chapter 10
A Renewed Spirit

The assignment given to me by God to write this book was laid upon my heart over two years ago. We don't always understand when God gives us an assignment. There was so much I didn't understand about this mandate. God called me unto His works, and I must be about my Father's business. I labored over this assignment because of my personal struggles. The assignment started with my desire to move to the next level of the ministry. I am blessed with many gifts. God has equipped me to be a teacher of His Word. I felt as if I had so much more to offer if I was afforded the opportunity. I prayed for God to take me to the next level. I was guilty of doing what I spoke of earlier. I was reaching for more, but I was not willing to let go of what I had in my hands.

During that time, I was the caregiver of several family members. I worked a full-time job, and I worked the ministries I had been assigned for that season. I had issues accepting the changing of seasons. I had issues with the changing seasons in my life. I sincerely could not understand the need for change. Although I have written three other books, this book has been the most challenging. I knew I had to write this chapter. This personal testimony is unusual because I usually don't write or share my personal struggles. I give God the glory for this season of change!

In that season, God took me through so many struggles. I was weak, dismayed, and confused. My struggles became unbearable, which caused me to question God's call on my life. All the struggles I dealt with were hard; the death of my mother was the hardest. I felt as if God had deserted me. I found myself in a hard place. I have comforted many who have lost loved ones. I was in need of being comforted, but I had no one to turn to. I was in a place where I no longer desired to study God's Word. When granted an opportunity to teach or preach, I would make excuses. When I did teach or preach, my messages felt empty. I did know without a doubt that God had not left me, and I continued in my prayer life. The death of my mother brought about changes in my life.

I could not understand—and refused to accept—my season of grieving. I was always filled with pride and always had control of my emotions. I was far from that proud person who was always in control. I was weak, confused, and disappointed. I didn't understand why I suddenly found myself alone.

As I communed with God, a song was placed on my heart. I couldn't get the song out of my mind. I researched the history of the song and the writer. In the late nineteenth century, W. B. Steven, a preacher in the little Crossroads village of Queen City, Missouri, was struggling with the death of his young son. He had ministered to many who had lost loved ones, but he found himself in this hard place. He wondered if he should keep preaching because his sermons felt hollow. He wondered how God could allow such a horrible thing to happen. He asked why good people suffered. Why me? Only God has the answers—I just needed to trust, obey, and release the things I cannot change.

Further Along
W. B. Steven

Tempted and tried, we're oft made to wonder
Why it should be thus all the day long
While there are others living about us
Never molested though in the wrong.
Further along we'll know all about it

Further along we'll understand why
Cheer up my brother, live in the sunshine
We'll understand it all by and by.

I didn't understand, but I knew God was in control. I may not understand it on this side, but I will one day. I realized that changes come because God allows them to come, and He doesn't make mistakes. I will understand it better by and by.

I believe my grieving season was the lowest and darkest time of my life. As a child, I was afraid of dark places. To get to certain locations in the city where I was raised, we had to go through a long, dark tunnel. Although I was in the car with my parents or grandparents, I was afraid. In the tunnel, things turned dark and dreary. After being in the tunnel for a while, we could begin to see a little light. The farther we traveled into the tunnel, the brighter the light got. Finally, we would come to the end of the tunnel and into the light again.

My season of grieving was like entering a long, dark tunnel. The tunnel was filled with darkness, but I kept pressing on. I felt as if God was not hearing my prayers, but I continued to pray. I began to see a hint of light, and I emerged into light. The season I was in had come to an end. It was living faith in my Lord and Savior Jesus Christ that brought me through.

When you are in God's army, you are equipped to fight the battle. Sometimes you may not see it and feel as if the battle is lost, but we must fight with the weapons God has given us. We fight and pull down strongholds. It's all about knowing, trusting, and having a relationship with the Father. "For my determined purpose is that I may know Him that I may progressively become more deeply and intimately acquainted with Him" (Philippians 3:10).

I understand what it means to suffer. Jesus suffered because it was the will of God, and it is God's will that we suffer with Jesus. We will suffer, but we must understand that suffering does not mean it's the end. Suffering is the beginning of new things. Jesus suffered, died on the cross, and arose to a new beginning. We suffer to renew our spirits. That's why it's so important to let go of the stuff we don't need. Release the junk so that a new spirit within us can be released. Christ stood alone when He died for our sins. We can never die as Christ did because He conquered sin and death for us. We cannot die as Christ did, but we can die to sin as Christ did. We can—and will—overcome with faith.

There comes a time in our lives when we go through periods of resistance and struggle. In order to move to a more powerful, purer way of life, we must oppose the old ways that ruled us, the habits and fixed patterns of our minds, wills, and emotions. The death of Christ does not keep us from sinning, but it does destroy the power of sin to take control. Releasing opens the door for a new and different life that is developed from the bottom to the top. The old foundations are no longer adequate for the higher level of a new life in Christ. Releasing raises us to new levels of living that we never thought we could have. The Holy Spirit releases these new levels.

Releasing junk releases a new spirit within you. We must allow changes in our lives. The life of Christ must take the place of the self-centered life. You can overcome because Jesus is now the life of your soul. There will never come a time that we can say, "I have no self to deny. I do not need to deny the self." We must maintain a continuous fellowship with Christ in order to ensure a continuous denial of self. We are purposed to do His will—not our wills.

We have been given the authority to stand against our enemies. In this season, the enemy is bringing a lot of obstacles into people's lives. It's time to stand with authority and say, "Stop, in the name of Jesus. You may have the ability, but you have no authority over my life."

"Behold, I give unto you power to tread on serpents and scorpions, and over all the power of the enemy" (Luke 10:19). The world needs broken men and women who are inwardly transformed to stand for God to make a difference. Brokenness makes wholeness. I realize I had to endure in order to understand that God often allows defeat to be followed by victory. He has a way of bringing His servants low before Him, humbling themselves under His mighty hand. He is able to raise them up in the next season. It is only by faith that we are able to see God as we are being disciplined as we walk through the seasons of life.

The world identifies one with the success and fame that they claim. God uses the meek and broken for His purpose. A Christian who is not truly broken cannot produce qualified disciples. Christlikeness is sometimes perfected through failed ambitions, plans, dreams, and hopes. Broken men and women are working to build God's kingdom—contrary to what men believe. Men believe that only the strong and successful can lead in the building of God's kingdom. It is in our weakness that we are strengthened. The world tries hard to change people from the outside in; true transformation is cleansing from the inside out.

In this present time, looking at the low values of many, it appears as if we are living in a time of darkness. Darkness has taken over the people in this land. The inability to deny oneself has everything to do with this time of darkness. Although few, there are those who have chosen to rise, shine, and stand in the glory of God. They have made the decision to release and grow.

The season of suffering brings true joy. The season of suffering cleanses our motives. The season of suffering equips us to do the will of God. The season of suffering equips us with great power. The season of suffering opens our eyes to the visions of God. The season of suffering brings to light a better ability to know and hear the voice of God as we follow after His will.

Christians are commissioned to live lives that are acceptable to God. We are not to concern ourselves with acceptance by others. We are challenged to change in this season. Change from the inside out; don't conform to this world. Mature into the character of Christ. Mature into a person who is able to walk away when others speak untruths about you. Know when to speak and when to be silent. Understand that God is the one and only true living God. Become someone who is able to stand through it all—no matter what season of life you are experiencing. Know when to release and allow growth to take place.

In this season, I have been transformed from the inside out, which has equipped me for better work. Are you ready—or are you choosing to stand looking back as Lot's wife did? Look back to the place where God is trying to remove you from. There is no way to move ahead while looking back. Stand and forgive your enemies as a marvelous witness to the world. Change from the inside out.

In my early years of the ministry, I took a course entitled, "The Crucified Life." I learned of the fallow life and the plowed life. The fallow life is people being content with themselves and the fruit they once bore. They do not want to be disturbed. They are steady, faithful, and always where they are supposed to be. They are fruitless. They have fenced themselves in and fenced God and His miracles out.

In the plowed life, the fences are torn down. The urge for the Holy Spirit, the pressure of circumstances, and the distress of fruitless living combine to humble the heart. This life is plowed, seeds are sowed, and fruit is bearing. Just as the rain falls on the seeds, God rains down His righteousness. I have chosen to live a plowed life; what will you choose? Change comes when we move into a season of growth.

My declaration in this new season is about my Lord and Savior. I stand boldly before my adversaries and follow my decision to walk the straight and narrow path of righteousness. I push the old self away and have no need to look back at the past. I will pursue my purpose, and I refuse to let up. I have chosen to move ahead at full speed. I will not back away from what is right. I have a clearer understanding about my redemption. I am redeemed, bought with the blood of Jesus, which secures my future. I refuse to allow others to force me to lower my standards or fail as I walk in my purpose.

I will no longer seek the approval of others or allow the status quo to justify who I am or whose I am. I will work with all the power within me to display the fruit of the Holy Spirit. I am not ashamed of the gospel of Jesus Christ. My walk is built on the foundation of faith as I lean on my Lord and Savior. My daily prayer is for patience and understanding as I labor with power on this battlefield.

Because everyone cannot and will not understand my mission, my friends will be few. I refuse to be bought out, compromised, or detoured. I refuse to sit at the table of negotiation with my adversaries. I am willing to sacrifice my all for His mission, giving myself over to my Master. I will not be silenced. I will not walk away. I will not let go of God's unchanging hand. I know that my last season on this earth will come one day. I will be dressed for the occasion. Because of my efforts here on this earth, "striving daily for perfection," He will recognize me.

I am so thankful for the season from which I have just emerged. I was carrying around extra baggage. That season lasted a year. I was beginning to think that season was my end. I fully understand it was my beginning. I am thankful because I know that the grace of God brought me through. I was allowing the sinful nature of pride to keep me from going through a healthy grieving season. When I humbled myself, I was able to understand the grieving process.

I don't want to dwell on it, but I went through that season to share so that others may be comforted. Grief is a process that can be managed, but it seldom ends. There will always be something around you that will cause an emotional upheaval. It is okay to cry, and it's okay to laugh.

We know in our hearts that our loved ones may be in a special place, but we miss them so much. I learned that it's important to acknowledge the pain because the pain is real. Don't hold your feelings in. Talk about what you are feeling. Get involved and get active; hiding the pain you are feeling does not bring about healing. On special days, look for new, less painful ways to celebrate. One of the most important things we need to remember is the love we have for our loved ones. Death does not diminish the value of the ones we love. Remember our loved ones' contributions to our lives; the value is enhanced and may lead to a heightened season of grief. Life goes on. It is impossible to overlook the memories that remind us of our losses. I had to learn how to nurture myself. As I learned to nurture myself, I learned to accept myself. Knowing yourself opens the door to mourning in ways that promote healing.

I believe the most fulfilling thing that happened to me during that season was that I died to self. My heart is happy that God saw me as worthy of suffering for Christ. I no longer concern myself with the need to record my works, and it is a joy to do the work of God. I am content in any situation because I know that any interruption in my life is the will of God. When I see my co-laborers in the ministry moving ahead, I honestly rejoice with them. I feel no envy. I don't question God. When others speak evil of me or overlook my gifts, I wait in silence for God to move on my behalf. I pray daily to endure the things of this world as Jesus endured.

By walking through my dark season with my hand in God's hand, I now have joy. I will not let anything separate me from the love of God. I am not perfect, but I have made a vow to strive for perfection. It is impossible to live as Christians unless we draw near to God by way of Jesus Christ. My heart and my soul are committed to the call of God on my life. I want nothing more than to do His will. I surrender my all to you, God.

Charles Wesley wrote a hymn that was derived from Leviticus 8:35. In that verse, the Hebrew priests were commanded to be faithful in their duties in the tabernacle. "Keep the charge of the Lord, that ye die not," Moses said. Each of us has a charge to keep. We must take it seriously. This hymn promotes service, Christian living, and holiness.

A Charge to Keep I Have

A charge to keep I have,
A God to glorify,
A never-dying soul to save,
And fit it for the sky.
To serve he present age,
My calling to fulfill;
O may it all my powers engage
To do my Master's will!

Arm me with jealous care,
As in Thy sight to live,
And O, Thy servant, Lord, prepare
A strict account to give!
Help me to watch and pray,
And on Thyself rely,
Assured, if I my trust betray,
I shall forever die.

We all have a charge to keep and a God to glorify. We have an immortal soul to provide for and a needful duty to our generation to serve. If we neglect our charges, our Master will soon call us unto Him to account for falling short.

> For I am not ashamed of the gospel of Christ: for it is the power of God unto salvation to every one that believeth; to the Jew first, and also to the Greek. (Romans 1:16)

Our enemies put most of the junk in our lives; sometimes we think those enemies are our friends. It's important to acknowledge that the enemy will strike out to destroy you and your purpose. I dedicate this to all who stand against God's purpose for man.

A Word to all my enemies

You are not really my enemies at all. In reality, you are some of the best friends I have.

I speak in sincerity and truth; there can be no perfection in the lives of God's elect without the chastising work of a real enemy. When a friend recognizes the good in me and understands me from the heart, this is true friendship. In my heart, I feel nothing but genuine love for them. But when I encounter an enemy who has done me nothing but wrong, I am stirred up and the spirit of defending myself, a spirit of "righteous indignation" overrides the sinful spirit within me. It is then I see in me the things I left behind—as well as the things I did not know were there before. I cry to God with a repenting heart, and He delivers me from the evilness I have seen in my life. The things that were hidden, lying dormant, until you, my enemy who I love, brought it to light with your slaying process. If it wasn't for you, God's called ones would never have had the glory of being mistreated for the Word of God. There is no way crowns of sorrow could have ever been worn by the early Christians without real enemies.

You know I cannot harm myself, and friends will not harm me either. No one but you, my enemy, is able to bring me to the cross. And it to the cross I must go, if I am to ever reach the glory of perfection extended by Lord and Savior. I have made so much progress, which must be done before entering unto the image of my lovely Jesus. I have so much to learn in all my trials. And my enemies are teaching me hard lessons. I now know without a doubt the road to glory is only by way of the cross. Without you, my way would still be lost. I believe that if you knew the good your evil deeds are working out in my life, you would not continue to support my success. The work of God is being done, and I love you because of all your efforts. "Love thy enemies" as He has commanded. I wondered how I could love my enemy, but you have taught me how. Because of you, I have grown in my walk with God, walking in increased grace, and partaken of His divine, loving nature.

Your work has been harsh and deceiving. There have been many times when I was hurt and painfully wounded. It is because of these trying experiences that I am able to come forth a better Christian and I am well on my way to being a survivor. I do not foresee you receiving any blessings for your lies and your schemes to destroy me. "Woe unto them through whom these offenses come." I want you to know that although your loss is great, it is on that great Day of Judgment that I can stand and say, "I will always love you and appreciate the part you had in perfecting this life of mine."

This day, I declare victory over my enemy; my nights are now days. I am redeemed and come forth as pure gold. I am delivered from the chains that bound me, freed from the gridlock of sin. I no longer allow anyone to convince me of what's right or wrong. I no longer carry the burden of all the negative things I thought I needed to grow. I have packed my bags and moved to the next level. I stand before God with my invitation to the great feast in hand. I long to be among the guest at the Lord's table. I encourage you to release the junk in your life, pick up your cross, and prepare to attend the great feast of the Lord. I thank God for the seasons in my life. I look forward to the next season with understanding that there is a season for everything. Praise God for change!

Personal evaluation Journal

As I approached the end of this assignment, God reminded me of something very important. God reminded me, that through all my struggles, I already had within me what I needed to move to the next level. It is the Spirit of God that brought me through my seasons. Are you on an emotional roller coaster? Are you ready to release to grow? Are you prepared to move to your next level? If your answers are "yes," I invite you to do a self-examination in preparation for your next level. God wants to use you, but you must be dressed for the occasion. Living a purposeful life starts within yourself. There are no right or wrong answers in this evaluation, only truthful answers. Changes can only be made after you know and accept what needs to be changed.

What is your purpose in life? What do you want to accomplish? I want so much to . . . .

- Have good health and be happy
- Be more like Jesus
- Make a lot of money
- Have a good family life

Read—2 Corinthians 2:18; Genesis 1:27

Describe the time you spend with God.

- I pray only when I am going through something
- I confess when I do wrong
- I meditate on scriptures daily
- I have a set time daily for my time with God

What do I need to develop a closer relationship with God.

_____

_____

_____

_____

Read—Colossians 3:16; Psalm 146:2

Think of your most painful moments. Were they greater than Jesus' suffering?

_____

_____

_____

_____

What do you feel when you read the words listed? Read—Romans 5:8

    Lonely

    Aching

    Sad

    Frightened

    Painful

    Disappointed

_____

_____

_____

_____

What do you desire to have a imitate relationship with God through Jesus Christ?

What is it that you realize you need to do to draw closer?

_____

_____

_____

_____

Do you fully understand the importance of being obedient?

Look up scriptures pertaining to be obedient, write one and memorize it.

_____

_____

_____

_____

Moving ahead means you must release something. Do you know what it is you need to release?

_____

_____

_____

_____

WORSHIP

Worship it to honor to reverence, to adore, and to render devotion and respect. Gods wants true worshippers—John 4:20-24

Are you a true worshipper?

_____

_____

_____

_____

What are some ways we can worship God?

I Chronicles 15:16-27_____

I Chronicles 23:5: 25:1-7_____

Psalm 149:3_____

Psalm 47:1_____

Psalm 134_____

Hebrews 13:15_____

David praised God because he knew God was worthy—2 Samuel

Moses praised God for being God—Deuteronomy 32:4

Barak and Deborah praised God for the willingness of the people—Judges 5:2

You should praise God because:
He is your help—Psalm 63:7

_____

For what He has done for you—Psalm 52:9

_____

Because of His Love for you—Psalm 57:10

_____

Because He is your covering in times of trouble—
　　Psalm 59:16

_____

Because His love is greater than all things—Psalm
　　63:3

_____

Because He hears your prayer—Psalm 66:20

_____

Because He is faithful—Psalm 71:22

_____

Because He is your burden bearer—Psalm 68:19

_____

Because there is victory in praising Him—Acts 16:25

_____

Because praise glorifies God—Psalm 5: 23

_____

It is when you praise God you are able to release your emotions and bring peace to your soul. Let praising be your lifestyle. Praise is what you must do!

I choose to live by the spirit and not in the flesh, I will do this by:

_____

_____

_____

_____

Are you planning to accept your invitation to the Wedding Feast?

Have you gotten everything in place to attend the great celebration?

Which describes your preparation?

- I am always thinking about His return and pray daily to keep myself pure for that day.
- I never really thought about it.
- I have mixed feelings.

Make of list of persons who have offended you. Mark 11:25 tells us we can forgive through prayer.

_____   _____

_____   _____

_____   _____

_____   _____

Read Matthew 18:22
      Luke 17:4
      Luke 23:34

Pride keeps us from living in the likeness of Christ. (Read the following scriptures and write the meaning.)

Psalm 31:23_____

Psalm 138:6_____

Proverbs 8:13_____

Proverbs 16:5_____

Proverbs 16:18_____

Isiah 13:11_____

1 Peter 5: 5-6_____

What would help you develop a servant's heart?

- Giving credit and glory to Christ
- Admit when you sin and ask for forgiveness
- Serve in any area you can
- Accept tasks others refuse
- Admit your weaknesses and ask for help
- Surrender your all to God
- Obey God even when God does not make sense to you
- Deny your desires
- Give to the needy
- Develop a heart of Jesus
- Walk in love
- Strive to reach perfection daily

TRACK YOU PROGRESS
NOTES